COTSWOLD GARDENS

COTSWOLD GARDENS

DAVID HICKS

AND SUZANNAH BROOKS-SMITH

PHOTOGRAPHS BY

ANDREW LAWSON

PHOENIX ILLUSTRATED

Contents

First published in 1995 by
George Weidenfeld & Nicolson Ltd

This paperback edition first published in 1998 by
Phoenix Illustrated
Orion Publishing Group, Orion House
5, Upper St. Martin's Lane
London WC2H 9EA

British Library Cataloguing-in-Publication Data
A catalogue record for this book is available from
the British Library

ISBN 0-75380-149-3

Copyedited by Jonathan Hilton
Designed by Harry Green
Printed and bound in Italy

For

C A R O L I N E B E A U F O R T

who made two marvellous gardens at Badminton

Since I was 18 years old the region of England known as the Cotswolds has been a special place for me. Sometimes I like to think that I must be some distant relation of Sir Baptist Hicks, whose body lies next to his ruined house at Chipping Camden.

The Cotswolds – its name derives from an Old English combination of *cots*, meaning sheep pen, and *wolds*, meaning rolling hills – always work their special magic. Perhaps it is the unspoiled, gentle landscape set with fine houses of mellow limestone; or is it the resplendent views over verdant countryside towards the fine market towns that border the region – Stratford to the north, Tetbury to the south and Woodstock to the east and Cheltenham to the west. These are still important Cotswold centres and, to its credit, the local council has recognized the beauty of this magnificent landscape and its fine buildings, and has kept at bay the uglier types of development that are so often associated with these last few years of the 20th century.

The micro climate of the Cotswolds is wet and windy during the winter and warm and breezy throughout the summer months. The soil, in general, has a good tilth and is well drained. This combination of natural beauty and good, workable soil has resulted in many noteworthy gardens, and so it is perhaps not surprising to discover that such famous plantswomen as Rosemary Verey and the late Alvilde Lees-Milne chose to garden in the region.

My own interest in gardening started when I was eight years old. It was at this point that my parents gave me a small plot, four feet square, in their own garden. Here I was given my head and allowed to grow a haphazard collection of garishly coloured annuals. Later I was to spend hours driving my mother, and the local nursery owner, to the point of distraction with unending questions about this type of shrub and that type of herbaceous perennial. I designed my first complete garden when I was 15. This was when we moved to Suffolk, and it was there that I first experimented with scale, which I believe is the single most important factor in creating a successful garden.

As a young man I was fortunate to live in the Temple at Stoke-by-Nayland, where I planted two formal 'rooms' of pleached hornbeams. Now, 40 years on, these trees have matured and the shape and form they

INTRODUCTION

David Hicks

ABOVE These stilt hornbeam trees were 10 feet high in 1980, and a year later I decided to back them with hornbeam hedging to make a solid wall of green. In winter, there are now Arthur Rackham-like combinations formed by the branches and twigs.

lend the 18th-century fishing pavilion are simply splendid. After my marriage in 1960 my interest in the garden as an extension of interior design strengthened. More and more, I started to plant for line and architectural structure. In my garden in Oxfordshire I created an essentially green-on-green space, using water and statuary as focal points.

In Portugal in 1986, I was architect, interior designer and garden designer for Mr and Mrs Amin Ghani. The house and garden style I created resonates with the simplicity and the strength of line I would describe as being representative of my signature. Both house and garden work one with another, and with the site, each part enhancing the other to make a complete design statement. Increasingly, my clients understand that no matter how small their outdoor space, it does not exist in isolation, and that the interior and exterior are inextricably linked.

RIGHT This box-edged garden is only 18 months old and yet it is already providing vital interest directly outside the south-facing drawing room. The stilt hornbeams backed by a hornbeam hedge have great architectural merit, even in winter, and the large stone urn works well in scale with the hedge behind.

BELOW Looking from the red room of copper beech to the pavilion – a 60th birthday present from my wife – the centrepiece of this vista is a simple stone fountain. This is mirrored by an identical fountain in the red room. In front of the Regency brick walls, I have planted standard limes with hedges beneath.

Another move of house in 1980, to an 18th-century farmhouse, co-incided with my own immersion in classical garden design. I looked in depth at the work of the great garden makers: Lancelot Brown, Humphrey Repton and William Kent. Similarly, I am fascinated by the work of great garden architects like Harold Peto, Sir Clough Williams-Ellis, Sir Geoffrey Jellicoe and Sir Edwin Lutyens, and so I have included Cornwell Manor, Buscot Park and Abbotswood as Cotswold examples of their work.

In terms of my knowledge of plants, I feel I owe most to those two great plantswomen Alvilde Lees-Milne and Rosemary Verey for expanding my repertoire of planting possibilities, and their own gardens are among the wonderful examples of Cotswold gardens to be found in this book. Overall, however, I think that my greatest influences were Nancy Lancaster and Roderick (Rory) Cameron. Nancy Lancaster understood so completely the subtle relationship between shape, colour and overall atmosphere that she was able to create in her several houses and gardens, all very different from each other, environments that are pure delight. She came into my life at the same time that I first saw Rory Cameron's garden at La Fiorentina at St Jean Cap Ferrat. Its outstanding qualities are its puri-ty and unerring sense of scale, both of which are used to such good effect within that exotic site.

The courtyard of Rory's garden was flanked by 30 matched orange trees – each rising from its own individual square of soil – all the trunks whitened with limewash. A wide grass path bordered by matched cypress-es ran down to the pool by the sea, intercepted at right angles by broad grass terraces. These were shaded by ancient olive trees, underplanted with acanthus and blue agapanthus. An Italianate loggia looked down on a vast chequerboard pattern of lavender, while, on the rocky promontory

BELOW LEFT This view shows a part of the beech hedge in winter, which gives shape to a number of rose beds on one side and a wide grass walk on the other. I do not like expanses of manicured lawn so I leave the long grass to go to seed before it is cut; it then makes a dramatic contrast when seen against the immaculately cut path on the expanse of lawn.

BELOW RIGHT To create the Gothic tent, I trained hornbeams within an iron framework made by the local blacksmith. It is now the focal point of a long grass walk flanked by beech hedges from the drawing room. Looking back, the folly can be seen in the distance standing guard over the secret garden.

beyond, bergenia thrived under umbrella pines. In the garden he grew flowers for the house: giant sunflowers for the salon, tuberoses for the all-white bedroom of his mother, the Countess of Kenmare, and pink lilies for the stone chimneypiece in the library. Rory Cameron was to create several other gardens, but the best was at Le Clos Fiorentina. His vision of the house and garden, and their splendid position, was total and uncompromising. Fortunately this garden is now owned by M. de Givenchy, who has retained all of Rory's ideas.

It was for this total cohesion that I started planning, even before I moved to our farmhouse in south Oxfordshire. The house was surrounded by several small, unkempt beds, half a dozen mature trees, a number of good old stone and local brick walls, and assorted farm buildings. The soil was poor and chalky and the landscape consisted of flat agricultural land with no natural vistas. My first priority was a very practical one, so with dozens and dozens of bags of compost and tons of well-rotted manure from our three horses, I set about improving the soil before I started planting the garden's living architectural structure.

OVERLEAF I designed my garden to give me pleasure throughout the seasons. My architecturally planted chestnuts frame a black-painted swimming pool, bordered with cobblestones. The chestnuts serve as a prelude to a vast vista, which stretches half a mile beyond. Since they are clipped hard every year, the branches of the chestnuts are dense and form intricate patterns in winter.

Looking out from the farmhouse, it was important to establish three vistas. From the drawing room, the south-facing vista is framed by tall pleached and clipped hornbeam hedges, reminiscent of John Fowler's immaculate essay in stilt hornbeams at the Hunting Lodge at Odiham. This is a 17th-century technique, so that the hornbeam seem to balance on stilts. The vista has a formal walk of manicured grass flanked by areas of controlled long grass. I find acres of closely cropped lawn remind me of golf courses. The walk is broken by a *clairvoyée* and gate and then, further on, is a Gothic tent of hornbeam. Beyond that, a quarter-mile-long *allée* of Spanish chestnuts directs the eye to the landscape beyond.

The west-facing vista from the dining-room, while different in character from the first, is a third of a mile long. Near the house are lines of standard horse chestnuts. These are planted in two L-shapes underplanted with further hedges of horse chestnuts, with two stone urns on plinths at the corners. There is also a swimming pool painted black with smooth stones set around it, so that it resembles a canal. Further on there is an avenue of horse chestnuts, and on either side I have planted thousands of hardwoods, which, when they have all matured, my grandchildren will enjoy.

From the library, the vista is less contrived – narcissii and crocuses planted in among rough grass to form a carpet around a large ilex. I have cut an *œil-de-boeuf* within a thick holly so that I can see if the gate is locked shut. Beyond is a ha-ha and then clumps of trees, planted in the Capability Brown tradition.

Within the garden, walls and hedges have been used to create individual 'rooms'. There is a secret garden room, for example, and to enter it you cross a drawbridge over a small moat surrounding a tower – a 60th birthday present from my wife. Inside, shrub roses tumble together in brick-edged beds, and poppies tussle for room with peonies, foxgloves and lilies. There is also a more formal arrangement of common box planted around terracotta pots, themselves planted with tree peonies.

My garden is 15 years old and the architectural framework is now well established. However, gardens are never static places and so I am continually creating new areas. Recently, for example, I established a red room, and in 1994 I laid out a box garden of geometric shapes, a walk framed by yew, and planted more than 14,000 English hardwoods.

What will never have space in my garden are herbaceous borders. When I plant flowers, they are never seen from the house and will only be used as cut flowers. My palette of plants has not really expanded in the last 40 years – I still like and use hostas, bergenias, angelica, acanthus, honeysuckle, roses and common box.

I now design gardens and lecture on the subject all over the world. My personal passion has become an integral part of my professional life. And one of the enduring delights of living where I do in south Oxfordshire is its proximity to so many important and charming Cotswold gardens.

I placed this stone urn, known as a Pope urn (after Alexander Pope) at the end of my secret garden as a focal point. I keep a ball of tarred string in each of my garden rooms, so if I need to tie something back quickly, it's there.

ABOVE The red room in winter retains its shape and structure. I have planted copper beech stilt trees underplanted with a copper beech hedge to provide a solid dark background to the stone urn with water. The urn is set against a stone wall flanked by wooden obelisks, which are smothered in 'Danse du Feu' roses in summer.

LEFT Within the red room there are four walls of copper beech and four dark green painted stands upon which the shocking pink rose 'Danse du Feu' climbs happily. In the arched alcove is a limestone urn fountain, against a stone wall. The water falls gently from the urn into a pool at the base.

ABOVE Peter Church, who maintains the garden with Paul Ballard, makes all the wooden garden structures to my design. I find lengths of hosepipe unsightly, so I designed a number of wooden hosepipe covers. These are not only attractive, they are also extremely practical. This is the type of detail I like to see in gardens.

RIGHT Fourteen years ago I planted these stilt hornbeam trees with the hornbeam hedge behind. I recently put 8 plastic terracotta-style pots in front of them. These are planted with globe artichokes and are divided and bordered by hawthorn, which I chose because it is practical, attractive and unusual as an edging plant.

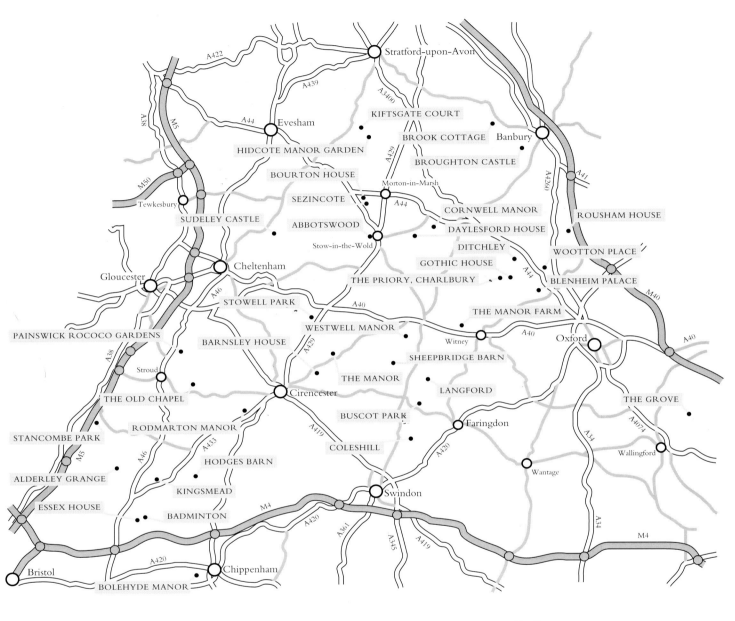

A422

A439

A3400

Stratford-upon-Avon

A44

Evesham

KIFTSGATE COURT

A38

M5

BROOK COTTAGE

Banbury

BROUGHTON CASTLE

A429

M50

HIDCOTE MANOR GARDEN

BOURTON HOUSE

A426

A41

Tewkesbury

SEZINCOTE

Morton-in-Marsh

A44

CORNWELL MANOR

ROUSHAM HOUSE

SUDELEY CASTLE

ABBOTSWOOD

DAYLESFORD HOUSE

Stow-in-the-Wold

DITCHLEY

WOOTTON PLACE

Cheltenham

GOTHIC HOUSE

A44

Gloucester

THE PRIORY, CHARLBURY

BLENHEIM PALACE

A46

STOWELL PARK

A40

M40

WESTWELL MANOR

THE MANOR FARM

A40

PAINSWICK ROCOCO GARDENS

A429

Witney

Oxford

A40

BARNSLEY HOUSE

SHEEPBRIDGE BARN

A38

Stroud

THE MANOR

THE OLD CHAPEL

Cirencester

LANGFORD

THE GROVE

BUSCOT PARK

A4074

RODMARTON MANOR

A419

Faringdon

A34

STANCOMBE PARK

A46

COLESHILL

Wallingford

A433

A420

M5

HODGES BARN

Wantage

ALDERLEY GRANGE

KINGSMEAD

Swindon

ESSEX HOUSE

M4

A420

A34

BADMINTON

A420

A361

A345

A419

M4

Bristol

Chippenham

BOLEHYDE MANOR

A420

10 miles

20 kilometres

THE
GARDENS

The Cotswolds, one of the loveliest regions in England, is home to a collection of spectacular gardens. Many of these gardens uphold traditions of design laid down by such well-known figures as Harold Peto, Sir Geoffrey Jellicoe and Humphrey Repton. It is in this setting that their gardens can truly be appreciated, as the beauty of the surrounding countryside is inextricably linked to the symmetry and elegance of the gardens.

ABBOTSWOOD
Stow-in-Wold Gloucestershire

Abbotswood is a 19th-century gabled Cotswold stone house, to which Sir Edwin Lutyens made some additions in 1901. Lutyens' first architectural priority was the fusion of house and garden. He considered garden architecture to be a continuation of the stylistic features of the house, and his understanding of the subtleties of scale and pattern throughout both the house and garden at Abbotswood has been used to great effect.

Now, nearly a hundred years on, the lily pool is still particularly successful, especially since its fountain forms part of the western elevation of the house. Although today the planting no longer balances the architectural lines of the

RIGHT The lily pool and fountain is a splendid feature of Abbotswood, clearly showing Lutyens' use of house and garden as two parts of a single idea. Here, the elaborate window of the west wall forms the upper part of the fountain, while the lower arch, set within the wall, ends in a shallow feeder basin.

BELOW Framed between skeletal branches can be seen Abbotswood, the 19th-century stone house to which Lutyens made some additions in 1901. Beyond the house, the Lutyens-designed garden pavilion can be clearly seen, set off to perfection by a foreground carpet of narcissi fringing wooded parkland.

series of formally linked gardens that Lutyens planned with such unerring skill, the bones of his garden still exist. The progression from the upper terrace walk to the surrounding parkland – taking in the flower garden, herbaceous border and sunken tennis court – is still magical. Your eye is drawn first to the Bourton Vale and then to the skyline that frames the entire picture.

But it is difficult in some places not to become aware of certain jarring details. The sunken tennis court, for example, now sports a small water feature with an even smaller statue rising from it.

The overflowing tubs of pink hydrangeas that once stood in straight, parallel lines flanking the lily pool are gone, and the planting in the flower

ABOVE The parterre of box-edged beds filled with pink tulips and forget-me-nots enfolds a weathered stone urn. Beyond, is Sir Edwin Lutyens' stone tennis pavilion in the corner of the sunken tennis court – the perfect place from which to view the terraces above and the more distant parkland.

RIGHT Rising from a bed of narcissi is an ancient oak. The gnarled trunk and groping branches give strength and natural architectural line to the cultivated March garden and the more distant pastures of spring lambs at Abbotswood.

BELOW In the woods near the house, a natural stream creates its own mini habitat. The blue scillas form a gentle backcloth for the *Lysichiton americanum*, the unfortunately named skunk cabbage. The foliage of this moisture-loving hardy perennial with an open spathe can grow to about four feet in height and will happily self-seed wherever conditions are favourable.

garden is not the clever tangle of colour it once was. Structurally, however, the garden still has huge merit and displays Lutyens' sure and certain grasp of the detail and harmony that need to exist between house and garden.

ALDERLEY GRANGE
Alderley, Gloucestershire

Alderley Grange is a fine 17th-century Cotswold house. When Alvilde and James Lees-Milne owned the Grange, Alvilde, a talented plantswoman, imposed a formal structure on the garden and combined this with an informal planting theme. Alderley Grange was her first major garden.

When Mr and Mrs Guy Acloque came to Alderley in 1975, Mr Acloque was not daunted by the thought of taking over where Alvilde had left off. Instead, the idea excited him. His knowledge of plants, especially the scented varieties, is comprehensive. On reflection, he believes that his interest was aroused as a small child by his mother's great friend and neighbour, Eleanur Sinclair Rhode. Guy Acloque remembers her as being 'the Rosemary Verey of the 1930s'. He also vividly recalls her garden as being 'full of bees and wonderful smells'. Eleanor Sinclair Rhode was a garden writer and plantswoman, whose special interest lay in aromatic plants. Her books were full of hints and plant lists. It was she who, with Leonard Messel, laid out Nymans – a garden of great renown.

With this background, Guy Acloque brought to Alderley his own planting bias, one that has served both to complement and enrich Alvilde's initial work.

LEFT A view through an 18th-century wall to the Lime Walk. Pleached and arched, the walk was planted by Alvilde Lees-Milne in 1963.

RIGHT Alvilde Lees-Milne laid out the original Herb Garden. The box-edged wedges centre on a stone urn in which Alderley Grange's present owner, Guy Acloque, has planted an exotic and aromatic curry plant. He has also planted a beautiful rose with deep pink double flowers that help to define the pale blue of the wisteria.

ABOVE Alvilde Lees-Milne planted this old-fashioned white rose that now cascades freely over the wooden 17th-century gazebo. The 'country Chinese Chippendale' wooden seat is thought to be original. The owners recently planted the foreground tulip tree, which Guy Acloque says is 'doing brilliantly'.

LEFT In the New Herb Garden the focus is mainly on scent, although large balls of clipped standard privet give an informal structure, as does the clipped pyramid of yew planted in the Italian stone pot at the centre.

On entering the garden, you are immediately confronted by an enormous bed of white 'Iceberg' roses, which Alvilde planted some 25 years ago. Another part of Alvilde's original garden contains the herbaceous borders and a most delightful 17th-century wooden gazebo with stone pillar. In reality, the herbaceous borders tend to be rather dominated by a collection of ageing, old-fashioned roses. Guy is slowly putting these beds to rights, and is resting the soil with phlox and delphinium.

From the herbaceous borders you enter a part of the garden known as the Lime Walk, and to the right of this is Alvilde's original octagonal Herb Garden. This area is now planted with a collection of taller herbs – angelica, sweet rocket and the larger varieties of marjoram. No garden is really complete, however, without the sound or sight of water to draw you on; and so, with this in mind, to the left of the Lime Walk there is an informal and quite intimate pond garden area. It is only when you move beyond the pond that you can more readily see the handiwork of Guy Acloque.

29

LEFT Opposite a large bed of 'Iceberg' roses, the border is edged with specimens of small-leafed box. Behind this bed is a myrtle given to Alvilde by Vita Sackville-West from her famous garden at Sissinghurst. Vita also gave Alvilde *Rosa* 'Sissinghurst Castle' (formerly known as *R.* 'Rose des Maures'), a rose that she found growing in the ruins of Sissinghurst when she took it over in the 1930s.

Where once a lilac hedge featured, this area of the garden – the new Herb Garden – now derives much of its form and structure from hawthorns (*Crataegus x lavallei* 'Carrierei'), which bear clusters of white flowers in May and black berries in autumn. On a more formal, architectural note, large balls of clipped, standard privet provide the perfect foil for the more informal, lower-level planting.

It is in the garden area opposite the greenhouse, however, that Guy Acloque's knowledge and love of aromatic planting has been allowed full rein. Aromatic-leafed plants, such as sweet-scented pelargonium; alecost, also known as costmary (a herb used by medieval monks to flavour their mead); camphor; balm of Gilead; and varieties of agastache have been planted to attract bees and butterflies. On a warm day, this part of the garden is the perfect place in which to savour the heady mixture of scents.

ABOVE This side view shows one of the borders planted by Alvilde Lees-Milne. It is an informal border containing various roses and catmint. The cottage gate divides the new kitchen garden from the more formal areas beyond.

BADMINTON
Avon

When the Duke and the late Duchess of Beaufort inherited the 'Big House' at Badminton in 1984, there was no garden. The intricate acres of late-17th-century parterres, topiary, fountains and walks that the first Duchess had laid out had all long since gone. And while William Kent's remarkable Worcester Lodge, one of the masterpieces of Georgian landscape architecture, is still to be seen, the overwhelming legacy of the past was the 18th-century 'naturalism' of Capability Brown.

The Duke and Duchess's first priority was to create a formal garden on the south front, close to the house. Using features already installed, such as the mellow stone walls of an elegant church, they added a yew hedge to mark out the perimeter of their new garden. Although the area is large, the garden's uniform structure and bold, lush planting create what can only be described as an intimate space.

The yew 'wings', which give shape to the series of low box-edged beds, make a deep green backcloth to the predominantly pink, white and grey planting used here, and there is also imaginative use of water within the formal planting nearest to the house.

The Duke is embarking on an adventurous planting programme in the park, too, with avenues of limes and chestnuts, as well as new woods. To the west of the house, the new ornamental vegetable garden is taking shape within the attractively mellow original garden walls.

LEFT The Duke and the late Duchess began their interest in gardening with their first house in Badminton village. Within its three acres they created the most splendid, quintessentially English garden. When they moved to the 'Big House' 11 years ago, there was no garden. Now the gardens at Badminton are simply ravishing.

ABOVE In the orangery on the east face of Badminton, a delicious climbing pink pelargonium, which obviously has a good head for heights, billows around the door frame. Its colour and size make it a superb specimen plant.

BARNSLEY HOUSE
Cirencester, Gloucestershire

Rosemary Verey moved into her pretty William and Mary Cotswold stone house in 1951. Now, more than 40 years later, she is a plantswoman with an international reputation.

The key to the success of her garden lies principally in its simplicity, although this is not to imply that it is in any way predictable. On the contrary, Rosemary approaches her garden with great care, exploring many styles and influences

BELOW The vegetable garden is an imaginative mixture of kitchen garden planting. Arbours of golden hops, trained dwarf fruit trees and standard roses combine to make this area an endless delight.

from traditional folk herbalists to the likes of Gertrude Jekyll and Vita Sackville-West.

Within her four-acre garden there are vistas , features and paths everywhere your eye falls. Visitors are rewarded, for example, by the sight of an entrancing 17th-century Doric temple (originally from Fairford Park) as well as a 17th-century Gothic summerhouse. There is also a fountain designed by Simon Verity.

ABOVE In front of the 17th-century Cotswold house, mature trees shade lawns planted with spring bulbs. Terraces slope away from the house to a path lined with cylindrical yews, whose solid, dark-green foliage emphasizes the fragility of the rock roses planted beneath. In the foreground are staccato junipers.

Rosemary Verey's charming knot garden consists of dwarf box with phillyrea styled on a 16th-century embroidery pattern. This is flanked by variegated topiary hollies softened by beds of lady's mantle, thus ensuring interest in both the horizontal and vertical planes. Her ornamental vegetable garden is yet another imaginative adaptation of an old idea, with its geometric, box-edged beds divided by low-maintenance brick paths and a symmetrical planting of unusual varieties of fruit and vegetables. Combinations of red chard, cabbages, lettuces, kale and standard gooseberries have been planted in attractive groupings to create design elements of line and harmony from these humble fruits and vegetables. Rosemary's planting is unerringly precise and her Cotswold garden is full of warmth and charm.

LEFT The shield pattern, designed in 1864 by Stephen Blake, is called the True Lover's Knot. There is no planting between its interlacing threads of box since, in the 16th-century, coloured earths and stones were favoured. Note the frame around the knot. The knot garden employs a disciplined use of planting to produce an intricate pattern based on a 16th-century embroidery design. Since there was not a great variety of plants available when these gardens first became popular, it is the design rather than the plants that is paramount.

ABOVE A room with a view – on to the herb garden, softened by a frame of variegated ivy. The simple box parterre was designed to be viewed to best advantage from above, and its pattern is interplanted with herbs to give both colour and scent near the house.

BLENHEIM PALACE
Woodstock, Oxfordshire

'We have nothing to equal this,' exclaimed King George III on passing through Vanbrugh's magnificent Triumphal Gate, the main entrance to Blenheim Palace.

Sir John Vanbrugh (1664–1726) was a soldier, actor, playwright, architect and garden designer. His greatest triumphs as an architect were undoubtedly Castle Howard and Blenheim Palace, which he was commissioned to build in 1705. He was apparently not formally trained, but in his 25 years as an architect he developed a Baroque style that was unique in England.

Vanbrugh's intention was that the surroundings of his buildings should be part of a well-orchestrated whole, and insisted that they include 'some plain but magnificent and durable monument'. At Blenheim, it was the bridge he built across the River Glyme that fulfilled this requirement. The main arch is 101 feet wide and there are 33 rooms within the stonework itself. The bridge was started in 1708 and its grandeur, scale and, of course, cost were to be the cause of a rift between Vanbrugh and Sarah, Duchess of Marlborough, who considered it an extravagant folly. Despite its cost, the bridge was never really in harmony with its surroundings, that is not until 50 years later when Capability Brown dammed the stream. The lake he thus created was of sufficient scale to make sense of Vanbrugh's extravagant vision.

Brown was the designer responsible for the layout of the park itself. In a stroke, he swept away the formal gardens at Blenheim in the belief that heroic and classical inspiration from

ABOVE The great palace of Blenheim was the Baroque masterpiece of the architect Sir John Vanbrugh. Queen Anne's treasury donated close to a quarter of a million pounds to the project – yet even this vast fortune proved insufficient to realize Vanbrugh's vision.

RIGHT Achille Duchêne's Italian Garden at the East Front of Blenheim Palace was once a Victorian shrubbery, but is now a gravel and dwarf box carpet of scrolls and arabesques. The garden, framed by yew, has an extravagant mermaid fountain at its centre.

BELOW The focal point of the Italian Garden is the circular pool, with the American Waldo Story's gilded mermaid fountain as its extravagant centrepiece. Although it is called the Italian Garden, this part of the grounds is much more French in character, echoing the early 18th-century work of Henry Wise of Blenheim.

RIGHT Duchêne's water terraces are to be found at the West Front of the Palace. The linked terraces abide by a strict formality – the upper terrace being square and much larger than the lower rectangular terrace, with its two pools guarded by a pair of carved lead sphinxes. The faces of these mythical creatures were modelled on those of the ninth Duke and his second wife, Gladys Deacon.

the past was a hindrance to the natural qualities of the site. In Brown's opinion, the impression of naturalness and permanence could be better realized by the manipulation of the broader landscape, such as his creation of the lake with its vast backdrop of beech woodlands. This piece of grand landscape architecture has been described as 'the one great argument of the landscape gardener'.

A view of Vanbrugh's bridge and Capability Brown's lake. The bridge was designed to span the valley of the little River Glyme, which flows through the park. The main arch is 101 feet wide and there are more than 30 rooms within the stonework, all unfortunately flooded when the river was dammed.

Closer to the Palace, the 20th century becomes more apparent. Here, at the East Front, is the sheltered Italian parterre garden. Its was commissioned by the ninth Duke of Marlborough before the onset of World War I. The Duke was determined to restore Blenheim to its former 18th-century glory by turning back the tide of neglect and decay that had been allowed to sweep through the Palace grounds by

RIGHT Yew topiary and standard trees in Versailles boxes soften the mellow stone façade of Vanbrugh's greatest work – Blenheim Palace. Vanbrugh finally left the project in 1716 after a row with the Duchess of Marlborough over the escalating costs of the work. When he returned to Blenheim to see his work finished, he was banned from entering.

BELOW The Column of Victory topped by its lead statue was raised to commemorate the victorious general, John, first Duke of Marlborough. Standing 134 feet high, it was finished in 1730, and can be seen from just about everywhere in the park. The central vista of the park runs straight from the Palace, across Vanbrugh's bridge, and terminates at the Column.

his predecessors. To this end he employed the French garden architect Achille Duchêne, although the venture was to be funded by the Duke's first wife, the American Consuelo Vanderbilt. Duchêne was also responsible for the restoration of Vanbrugh's North Court, the stone paving of which Brown had grassed over.

After the end of World War II, Duchêne turned his attention to creating the spectacular water terraces situated between the west façade of the house and Capability Brown's lake. The terraces were in response to the problem of bringing balance and harmony to the huge panorama of the lake, the landscape beyond and the house behind. The Duke, obviously pleased with the result, described the terraces as 'magnificent . . . far superior to the work done by Le Nôtre at Versailles'.

BOLEHYDE MANOR
Allington, Chippenham, Wiltshire

Bolehyde Manor was built in the late 16th century as the guest house to Malmesbury Abbey. Gables, and mullioned windows were added to this essentially Jacobean structure in the 17th century. Now, the Manor is first and foremost a comfortable family home.

When the present owners moved in about nine years ago, they found that the garden had some well-established yew hedges providing form and structure and, in the Long Walk, there was an assortment of mature shrubs, several lilacs and a cherry tree. There were also eight neat beds of hybrid tea roses. This reminded the owners so much of the type of municipal planting commonly seen in parks and other public spaces that they jokingly named this area of their three-acre garden Regents Park. This name has

persisted even though the once ordered beds are now gone and have been replaced with box-edged areas overflowing with a wide and varied assortment of plants.

The garden has been laid out in stages and is basically informal in its approach and structure. The owners view it as an extension of their lifestyle, and so each feature – the black swimming pool, tennis court and croquet lawn – has been designed as an integral part of the whole garden area.

Surrounding the garden is a working farm, so a new ha-ha (sunken wall) has been built to dissuade the cows and pigs from mingling too freely with the family. The original moat has been repuddled with clay and is now stocked with hardy carp.

RIGHT At one end of the croquet lawn, an ancient wisteria climbs the original 16th-century chapel wall. The clematis 'Perle d'Azur' climbs in amongst the wizened branches of the wisteria, prolonging the flowering season in this part of the garden in the process.

LEFT In the Lady's Garden, square-cut yew hedging underplanted with hostas make a green room for the statue of a lady whose nose was destroyed by a cricket ball. Her battered face is now turned towards a window cut into the yew wall allowing her gaze to fall on the apple orchard and Chippenham beyond.

BOURTON HOUSE
Bourton-on-the-Hill, Gloucestershire

The present Bourton House was built by Alexander Popham in the early 17th century on the foundations of an earlier structure. The magnificent stone tithe barn, built in 1570 by Richard Palmer, still remains.

When Mr and Mrs Paice moved into Bourton House in 1983, the stone garden walls were still standing. These are thought to have been built around 1800 when the estate land was sold to its nearest neighbour, Sezincote. There was also a massive, 12-feet-wide yew hedge and a jungle grew unchallenged in what had been the old kitchen garden. There was one herbaceous border remaining, which was said to have been designed by Lanning Roper, but this was completely overgrown.

Little inroad was made in the first year, until Paul Williams arrived as gardener. Then he and Mrs Paice set about rebuilding the garden, keeping Mr Paice's favourite plants firmly in mind.

ABOVE This imposing, early-17th-century stone house has had a chequered past – one of the early owners was said to have been implicated in the hanging of three innocent men. The Chinese parterre garden was inspired by a pattern of Chinese trellis furniture.

LEFT The Chinese trellis parterre garden is box-edged, with green planting within the pattern. The metal frame of the arbour provides support for the ivy, which was planted only four years ago. By next year it should cover the entire frame, creating an imaginative, living structure.

RIGHT A view of one of the new borders at Bourton House. Although Mrs Paice says she loves 'straight lines', the hard edges of the garden are softened with pretty borders. The planting and colour combinations here show a restrained and imaginative handling of a border.

Drastic action was needed and the massive yew hedge was taken back to its stumps. The hedge now is thriving and is perfectly proportioned. The neglected kitchen garden was also taken in hand and has been transformed into an inventive topiary garden, while species of large box are being trained to form buttresses along the wall with pleached holm oaks behind.

The box-edged parterre garden is a triumph, and the intricate, growing pattern was based on a design taken from a book of Chinese trellis furniture details. The entire garden is predominantly green-on-green, and it relies on bold architectural shape and form for its considerable impact. Where colour is used, it is controlled and immensely successful as a result.

LEFT This was once a neglected and overgrown walled kitchen garden. Now it is a striking topiary garden of clipped box spirals, pyramids and globes. Against the early-19th-century stone walls, clipped box forms green buttresses. Throughout the garden, colour is used sparingly and to great effect.

ABOVE Mrs Paice attributes her gardener, Paul Williams, with a wide knowledge of plants and an uncanny and unfailing sense of what looks right together. The colour combinations here work particularly well. Mrs Paice favours texture and form in plants and often introduces specimens with strong architectural interest.

BROOK COTTAGE
Alkerton, Oxfordshire

The village of Alkerton clings to the side of a steep escarpment overlooking a small Cotswold valley. When the present owners of Brook Cottage, Mr and Mrs Hodges, moved here in 1963, they were to find not so much a garden as just a series of steep, open fields. The transformation is now complete, and Brook Cottage today can be found set among four acres of lush gardens – trees and plants all thriving in the alkaline soil.

Mrs Hodges came to Brook Cottage as a 'London gardener'; but as she and her husband learned more about what they liked from books and other gardens, the size of their own plot gradually increased. Various levels have been carved from the naturally sloping terrain, which the Hodges have used to great advantage by planting more than a hundred varieties of old-fashioned shrub roses. These are liberally intermixed with modern shrub roses to prolong the flowering season. They also introduced ground-cover roses to clothe the steepest banks, which would otherwise be difficult to maintain.

Their white border garden calls for a disciplined and restrained planting scheme, and the Hodges have used different textures, shapes and heights to dramatic effect. White delphiniums stand tall amid soft white valerian, half-hardy white penstemons, white campanulas and a pretty, shrubby artemisia with its silvery coloured leaves.

Beside the pond created by the Hodges, *Hosta sieboldiana* var. *elegans*, with its pale lilac flowers in July and August, euphorbia and generous clumps of lady's mantle (*Alchemilla mollis*), thrive in the boggy soil at the margins.

ABOVE Around the pool are abundant plantings of moisture-loving plants, such as hostas, irises and *Primula florindae* with *Euphorbia griffithii* 'Fireglow' An elegant garden seat, made by the Hodges' son, invites you to linger in the cool shade. Below the pond is the tennis court, well hidden by plants and a vast white cherry tree.

RIGHT Glimpsed through a gated opening, this border is framed by an old Cotswold stone wall. Height has been given to the planting by the presence of a weeping silver pear, and roses and foxgloves stand above the low-growing sea thrift. The yellow broom smells deliciously of pineapple.

ABOVE This white border is
wonderfully disciplined, and
the interest that the towering
white foxgloves and delphiniums give with their irregular
heights and spacings punctuates the silver of the other
foliage. At the base of this
imaginative border are small
daisies, with a spiraea and
white clematis behind.

RIGHT The white metal seat
designed by the garden
owner's son, surrounds an
ancient apple tree at the end
of the white border. The
frothy white valerian is in
dramatic contrast with the
tree trunk. Mrs Hodges
describes the perfect lawn as
being 'quite ghastly because
none of it is flat'.

BROUGHTON CASTLE
Oxfordshire

Built in 1306 of the warm, gingery coloured stone typical of the area, Broughton Castle has been the family seat of the Fiennes since the mid-15th century. Both the Castle and gardens are enclosed by a fine moat and, when viewed from the adjacent park, offer one of the most romantic settings to be found anywhere in the Cotswolds.

When the present Lord Saye and Sele inherited the property in 1968, the gardens were in need of restoration. For help with this project, the late Lanning Roper was brought in to act as adviser. The centrepiece of the gardens you now see at Broughton is without doubt the Ladies' Garden, which was originally established by the wife of one of the Castle's tenants at the end of the last century. The box-edged parterre is filled with old-fashioned roses, predominantly whites and pinks, while generously proportioned beds, overflowing with foxgloves and campanulas, abut ancient stone walls. The walls provide not only protection from the wind, which can be a problem in the Cotswolds, but also reflected light and warmth for the plants beneath.

An extraordinary border runs the 200 yards between the gatehouse and the southern corner of the Ladies' Garden. It is very much in the Jekyll tradition, and Broughton's last gardener, Randal Anderson, planted it with great sensitivity and imagination.

Although largely a conventional garden, the intelligent use of plants, both formally and informally arranged, allows it to fit seamlessly into the surrounding countryside; an area of park and farmland stretching to distant, gently rising hills.

RIGHT These ancient walls are swathed in old-fashioned roses intermingling with honeysuckle. The scent in summer is heady. In this view, *Rosa* 'Albertine' is underplanted with pink double peonies, *Salvia sclarea* and *Euphorbia polychroma*. From here, there is a delicious view of the great house and its comfortable relationship with its surrounding gardens.

LEFT The stone window and seat give an inviting glimpse of the garden beyond. The use of a welter of traditional English flowers, including old roses, sweet rocket and lady's mantle, produces a sense of luxury.

The celebrated Ladies' Garden was first laid out in the late 19th century by Lady Gordon Lennox, while she and her husband were tenants in the Castle. It has barely changed in the intervening years. The focus of the garden is a bowl densely planted with diascias and verbenas. The garden makes a tight, geometric statement surrounded by herbaceous borders.

LEFT In this effective wall planting, massed foxgloves strike a dramatic frame for the wide moat and ancient clumps of trees in the parkland beyond. The moat is set well back from the Castle grounds and creates a rectangular island.

ABOVE At the entrance to the Ladies' Garden, the famous rambling wichuraiana rose 'Albertine' is seen in full flush. Its pale pink blooms have a charming, rather haphazard arrangement of petals. Here it is underplanted with santolina. Beyond the Ladies' Garden the castle wall glows in the summer sunshine.

LEFT The Ladies' Garden with the Castle itself forming one of the garden walls. The shaped foreground beds here are home to pale pink old-fashioned roses, while in the borders the deeper pinks and purples make an interesting contrast.

ABOVE Broughton Castle's garden is essentially romantic, largely due to Randal Anderson's planting, which is very much in the Jekyll tradition. Although Anderson is an American, he has managed to capture perfectly the spirit of an English country garden.

BUSCOT PARK
Faringdon, Oxfordshire

Buscot Park is thought to have been designed in 1780 by the then owner, Edward Loveden Townsend. When the first Lord Faringdon bought the house at the end of the 19th century, he enlisted the garden architect Harold Peto to remodel the approach to the house and the gardens.

Peto was a leading exponent of the formal Renaissance revival style of garden design. In a famous and outspoken statement he declared that: 'flowers should occupy an entirely subordinate place in a garden, as they did in the classic Italian examples.' A sentiment with which I totally agree.

RIGHT Harold Peto's canal narrows at the crossing point of his small Italianate bridge, as can be seen in this view that looks back to the stone stairway towards the house.

LEFT The original kitchen garden, with its vast 18th-century brick walls, has been completely revamped. Here, the late Peter Coats installed a walkway bounded by 18-feet-wide mixed borders, planted with well-proportioned clumps of shrubs, trees and perennials. In this autumn picture, the tree *Robina pseudoacacia* 'Frisia' has been under-planted with the plum-leafed shrub *Berberis thunbergii* 'Rose Glow' and the perennial *Sedum* 'Autumn Joy'.

ABOVE A fountain punctuates Peto's water garden with its series of stone-edged pools and canals meandering down to the 22-acre lake in the distance. The severely clipped symmetrical yew hedging and Irish yews are an integral part of Harold Peto's formal Italianate design.

LEFT At the centre of the newly designed Four Seasons Garden, within the walls of Edward Townsend's original kitchen garden, is the stone-balustraded fountain where four box-edged tunnels are starting to take shape. Most unusually, Judas trees (*Cercis siliquastrum*) are being trained into fans that will eventually cover the arch. The garden's name derives from the 'classical statuary' in each corner, depicting the four seasons, designed by Frank Foster in fibreglass.

When Peto started at Buscot in 1904 there was already an extensive walled garden, two lakes and a sizeable park in existence. In order to link the house with one of these lakes – a 22-acre expanse of water – Peto devised a splendid water garden.

Buscot's formal walk consists of a chain of stairways, paths and pools for the greater part of its length. To achieve this grand procession, the path has been cut through a wood and is enclosed by clipped yew and box hedges. Here and there fountains play, and to enchant the eye a miniature cascade tumbles water beneath a small bridge. Carved into the yew hedges are niches furnished with classically inspired statues. The effect is of a fine Italian *allée*. To the west of the house, Tim Rees has redesigned the original kitchen garden as the Four Seasons Garden using, as with all the garden areas at Buscot Park, line and form as his guiding principles.

THE CLOCK HOUSE
Coleshill, Swindon, Wiltshire

The Clock House used to be the original stone laundry and brew house of Coleshill House, designed by Roger Pratt in 1650 and gutted by fire in 1952. The late Michael Wickham moved into the Clock House within Coleshill Park in 1961 and started work on the garden, which then was nothing more than six acres of weedy field. Over the last three decades, the garden has been grown organically and it is now a series of garden 'rooms'.

Michael Wickham was a painter and photographer, and the artist's eye can clearly be seen in the garden he created with his wife, Denny. While line and form dictate the garden areas, it is not an architectural garden. Lady Mary Keen, the writer and plantswoman, once said to Michael Wickham, 'What I like about your garden is that it all looks slightly out of control'.

The garden is romantic and full of imaginative plantings, but it is the House-Plan Garden that I find most satisfying. Two rows of limes flank the central lawn where the English Palladian house once stood (it was razed to the ground after the fire). Here Michael and Denny Wickham accurately outlined the original house in box-hedging and filled in the 'walls' with annuals and roses. A passage of lavender runs down the centre of the 'house' and the 'rooms' have gravel floors, which are now covered with self-seeded poppies and thyme. In many ways this is an unconventional garden, the result of one man's strong, painterly vision.

This avenue of limes, which separates the garden from the lawn, was planted in 1968 by Michael Wickham. A carpet of cow parsley and daisies soften the straight lines the trees present. To the right can be seen the edge of the House-Plan Garden, which outlines the beautiful English Palladian house razed to the ground after a fire in 1952.

CORNWELL MANOR

Chipping Norton, Oxfordshire

The present façade of Cornwell Manor dates from 1750, but the house and land were mentioned in the Domesday Book. When Peter Ward acquired the Manor, the village stream had already been harnessed into canals running through the garden, by architect Sir Clough Williams-Ellis. As well as a natural lake, there are two others, possibly created by Williams-Ellis since they are reminiscent of the strong architectural style and love of classicism that the creator of the village of Portmeirion in Wales brought to his designs.

However, it was Simon Baring who devised the terraces and the linked gardens and also the planting of the 12-acre garden. This was in 1959, and much of it remains intact today.

The formal area of the garden is bordered by a ha-ha, and there are areas bright with daffodils in the pastures. In one of the informal areas, a carpet of blue scilla in March mirrors the spread of the old beech tree under which it grows.

Everywhere, the gardens are studded with mature trees: *Acer griseum*, with its peeling bark and glossy mahogany-coloured wood; *Magnolia*

BELOW The garden in front of the east façade of the 18th-century Cotswold stone house was designed by Simon Baring for Peter Ward in 1959. The formal lines and Italianate feel of the garden make a charming foil to the house. The standard wisteria is an unusual touch and the peonies planted within the box are a delight.

ABOVE Sir Clough Williams-Ellis (1883–1978) entitled his memoirs *Architect Errant*, and his creation at Portmeirion in Wales seems to suggest that he saw himself outside the establishment. However, his design of the system of canals that flows through Cornwell Manor and terminates in a series of lakes, shows his strong treatment of the landscape.

LEFT A pond punctuates the Williams-Ellis water garden at Cornwell Manor. The canal system is reminiscent of Harold Peto's large Italianate water feature at Buscot Park. Here, however, there is less formal planting, although symmetry has been used to accent the form of the canals and ponds within the garden.

69

obovata with its stunning pink-flushed cream flowers; the evergreen *Osmanthus delavayi* and its clusters of heady scented, tubular-shaped flowers in April; and the winter-flowering witch-hazel (*Hamamelis mollis*). All have been planted with careful consideration of colour and form.

In front of the house's east façade is the formal garden, divided into six parterres surrounded by strips of box with clipped box balls at each corner. At each centre is a 35-year-old clipped Portuguese laurel. Cornwell Manor today is a tribute to the skill of successive gardeners.

ABOVE This statue sits at the centre of one of the parterres in the East Formal Garden. The overhanging trees soften the neat lines of the lawn and clipped box hedges.

RIGHT On the south side of the formal garden the level changes. Shaped yews and two stone balls at the top of the stairs invite you towards the densly planted herbaceous border and the gently slopping lawn, dotted with mature trees.

DAYLESFORD HOUSE
Stow-on-Wold, Gloucestershire

Daylesford House was built in Hornton stone by Samuel Pepys Cockerell, the architect responsible for Sezincote. It is in the Indian style of architecture and was commissioned by Warren Hastings on his return from a career dogged by financial and political intrigue in India, where he as the first governor-general, and then, later, in England.

Hastings was an energetic man, and with money bestowed on him by the East India Company after his retirement, he undertook a massive project encompassing both the house and its gardens and park. One of his first acts was to employ John Davenport to begin construction of two new lakes and an orangery – the Gothic Greenhouse.

After Hastings, each of Daylesford's many owners affected changes. When the present

RIGHT On the west terrace is the parterre, adapted from a Mogul pattern in the Victoria and Albert Museum, London. The pattern is punctuated by box spirals and interplanted with muscari and tulips. Along the stone balustrades in summer grow the roses 'Alberic Barbier' and 'New Dawn'.

ABOVE A view of Daylesford House and the Gothic Greenhouse, which is attributed to John Davenport. This beautifully proportioned, rectangular building, with its crenellations and Gothic finials, overlooks the upper lake and the Evenlode Valley below. Today it houses a wide variety of citrus fruit trees.

LEFT The rose garden was planted on a raised and terraced part of the walled garden and painted trellis, made of wood and metal, is the framework for a cascade of white, heavily scented roses.

BELOW A seat surrounds a Japanese lantern at the centre of the walled garden. Fruit trees and roses will eventually clothe the arches across the path beyond. In the surrounding beds, semiwild cottage-garden flowers, such as larkspur and nigella, flourish in the spirit of companion planting.

owners bought the property, they set about the task of restoring both house and garden to a high standard.

Now the garden design incorporates a wonderful simplicity of structural lines and good, imaginative planting. This can immediately be seen at the front door of the house, where the portico is flanked with thick hedging within which sit two enormous terracotta pots of standard strawberry trees (*arbutus*). These, in turn, are underplanted with box.

Away from the house, you discover a private, romantic dell of rhododendrons and an ash wood, which, in May, is thickly carpeted with nodding heads of bluebells. The lakes are crystal clear and fed by natural springs.

DITCHLEY PARK
Woodstock, Oxfordshire

Ditchley House was built for the second Earl of Litchfield by James Gibbs between 1722 and 1740. Its austere Palladian exterior, however, is in stark contrast with its elaborate interiors, which were devised by William Kent.

The house stands on high ground overlooking the Glyme Valley, in a wooded landscape and park – complete with lake and temples –

BELOW This view encompasses what is left of Sir Geoffrey Jellicoe's formal garden at Ditchley Park. Lawn has replaced almost all of the geometric parterre. However, the little that remains gives you an idea of the scope of the original concept. The yew hedges and pleached lime walks are much as they were when planted in 1935.

RIGHT Looking upward from the bathing pool, which is designed to be screened from the west façade of the house by a wall of fountain jets, Nancy Lancaster's beloved pleached lime walks and framing yew hedges stand sentinel beside the lawn, which was once the grand Italian Garden by Sir Geoffrey Jellicoe.

designed by Capability Brown in 1770. Between the wars, Ditchley was bought by Mr Ronald Tree and his American wife Nancy Lancaster.

One of the first things the Trees did was to employ Geoffrey Jellicoe (now Sir Geoffrey) to design the areas around the house. This was Jellicoe's first large-scale commission and his work here has been described as 'the last major English garden to be designed in the Italian style'. Jellicoe's ability to balance and harmonize classical and modernist ideas underpins his garden design.

At Ditchley, his vision and enthusiasm were matched by that of the owner, Nancy Lancaster, and together they set about creating a geometric garden stretching away from the terrace immediately below the west front of the house. His original centrepiece, an elaborate rectangular parterre, has subsequently been removed and replaced by an area of plain lawn – a great loss. But the yew hedges and pleached lime walks still survive today.

Nancy Lancaster was a famous society hostess and Ditchley Park became Sir Winston and Lady Churchill's weekend refuge during the years of World War II. Her inimitable flair and exceptional taste made all her houses and gardens something special.

ESSEX HOUSE
Badminton, Avon

Essex House stands within the totally unspoilt village of Badminton. When James and the late Alvilde Lees-Milne moved in 25 years ago there was no garden at all, and so Alvilde set about creating one from scratch. Although small by comparison with her previous gardens, she managed to include all her favourite aspects of design, while maintaining a feeling of space and order. The effect is enchanting.

In the area of garden closest to the house the planting is intensive. This is balanced by an

RIGHT Shaped box-edged beds give form and symmetry along the axis of the garden. The soft planting gives Alvilde Lees-Milne's garden the Englishness that is so admired.

BELOW Painted a rich cream colour, Essex House makes a warm backdrop for the garden. The box-edged beds are planted with *Stachys byzantina*, thyme, campanulas and helianthemum, with standard hollies 'Golden King' at the corners of the beds.

open, square area of grass at the centre of which she used cones and balls of clipped box to achieve a series of formal highlights to guide the eye through the garden.

Alvilde Lees-Milne's design instinct was that a certain amount of formality is necessary in a small garden, so even apparently random plantings of shrub roses are, in fact, carefully and strategically positioned. Elsewhere in the garden she used John Treasure's idea of threading clematis in and out of shrub roses in a naturalistic fashion to admirable effect.

Where space is limited, it is sometimes necessary to bend the natural habit of plants to suit your will, and so you will find standard honeysuckles used as structural plants. Although I do not care for variegated box, Alvilde has included six pairs of variegated box cones along the central stone path. These create an axis of the garden and the symmetry they impose works well in the context of her garden.

Although Alvilde Lees-Milne is now sadly dead, her imaginative planting and serene gardens continue to charm and delight all those who see them.

ABOVE More roses and, as Alvilde described them, 'herbaceous things'. The rose in the foreground is a useful one, *Rosa* 'De Rescht' – a Persian rose of a rich crimson colour, very free flowering and virtually trouble free.

RIGHT Alvilde Lees-Milne was a well-respected gardener and plantswoman all her adult life. It is little wonder that people such as Mick Jagger used her to design the garden of his château in France. She was an erudite and a beautiful woman who gave great care and love to her gardens. The perfection she created is clearly seen in this romantic corner of her own immaculate garden.

GOTHIC HOUSE
Charlbury, Oxfordshire

Andrew and Briony Lawson have designed their garden to have no distinct beginning or end – no easy task with just a third of an acre behind their attractive Cotswold village house. Ten years ago, when the Lawsons moved into Gothic House, there was an old orchard, a large yew tree, and very little else.

Their first job was to clear the original garden and to start laying down the structure of their new one. Andrew Lawson, a painter and leading garden photographer, has used trellis to provide height, planting to flesh out the design, and painted effects and Briony's own sculptures to

ABOVE In winter, garden interest centres mainly around the trees and the structural elements that have been introduced. This apple tree is a survivor from the original orchard, and the Moorish-inspired trellis was designed to make a semicircle around it. Rather than making the garden look small, the trellis wall and arches draw you on to another area full of surprises.

RIGHT At the bottom of the garden at Gothic House, and behind the Moorish trellis, you discover a tiny pleached lime walk, which leads you to a torso sculpted by Briony Lawson. The green tripods act as host to clematis and sweet peas, while railway sleepers create raised beds, down which flowering alpines and ferns cascade.

LEFT Giant hogweed grows from a chimney pot under-planted with tulips, tall 'White Triumphator' and peony-flowered 'Mount Tacoma'. This path leads to the central and most imposing structure found the garden – the Moorish trellis.

enhance the feeling of depth and distance. You
are not meant to be taken in by the false perspectives created or the *trompe l'œil* view of the
Hartland Peninsula – Briony's birthplace in
North Devon – but they do help to set the
mood of the garden. Her sculptures emerge
from among the plants, almost as an after-
thought, and there is a tangible sense of fun and
mystery everywhere you look.

Across half the garden's width is a trellis framing the surviving apple tree from the original
orchard. This gives a focus to the far end of the
garden, which now has a tiny pleached lime
walk as well. Colour is Andrew Lawson's greatest passion, and he admits to using masses of
bulbs and annuals each year, trying out different
colour relationships. It is this artistic and painterly approach that has bestowed such wit on this
relatively small garden.

HIDCOTE MANOR
Chipping Campden, Gloucestershire

As one of the most influential gardens in England to be created this century, Hidcote Manor had an inauspicious start. It was bought for Lawrence Johnston in 1907 by his mother, when it was nothing more than bare farmland, situated 600 feet up at the northern end of the Cotswolds in an exposed position, and on thin, chalky soil.

But here, over the next 40 years, Lawrence Johnston created a garden made up of distinctive 'rooms'. It seems likely that he devised these rooms as a response to the difficulty of the site. By far the greatest part of the 10 acres that the garden now covers was open field, and the hedges you see today were planted to give shelter to the plants. Thus, Hidcote became a garden of many hedges. But not content to have them as mere protection, Johnston used combinations of beech, box, yew, holly and hornbeam to create tapestry backcloths.

His use of tall hornbeam hedging along the length of the 300-yard-wide grass avenue, known as the Long Walk, is most impressive. Indeed, these hedges, sharply clipped and geometrically exact, are the principal feature of that part of the garden.

Although he did not have any background as a gardener, Johnston rapidly acquired the skills and knowledge of a plantsman. In the period between the wars, he expanded the terrain across hill-top farmland, and realized his personal vision of landscape gardening – a fern garden and wooded area planted with holm oaks.

In the parkland at the garden's southwest corner, there is a lush planting of water-loving plants, such skunk cabbage, astilbes, bergenias, giant lilies, and the huge-leafed *Gunnera manicata*, which is suitable only for large sites.

Within the main garden, each room focuses on one idea or feature, such as a particular colour or a single species of plant. Hence their names – White Garden, Fuchsia Garden, Red Borders, Stilt Garden, Pillar Garden, Terrace Garden, Mrs Winthrop's Garden (Johnston's

The White Garden is seen here with its crisp, box edges, while plump topiary birds rest peacefully on their plinths. The thatched cottage seen in this view is a village cottage outside of the garden.

LEFT The Long Walk comprises a wide avenue of perfect velvety grass bordered by shaped hornbeam, clipped with geometric precision. It is 300 yards long and makes up the western boundary of the garden. The vista at the end of the Long Walk is exceptional; down the valley to Chipping Campden, Broadway and the Malvern Hills.

ABOVE A lilac-encircled view through to the Fuchsia Garden and Bathing Pool Garden. Two large topiary birds stand sentry on stout pedestals of yew and a plain rectangular doorway cut into a solid yew pediment can be glimpsed.

LEFT The Stream Garden is lushly planted, creating a jungle-like feel, and many of the trees, shrubs and herbaceous plants come from China and Japan. Included in this view are candelabra primulas, hostas, ferns and the scalloped leaves of *Darmera peltata*, with birch and maple trees beyond.

RIGHT Mrs Winthrop's Garden is based on her favourite colour – yellow. The small terracotta-coloured square has brick paths and is lined with yellow-leafed *Lysimachia nummularia* 'Aurea' and lady's mantle.

BELOW The Pillar Garden seen in winter. In summer, these 22 clipped yews stand above splendid varieties of peonies, whose flowers are in a range of pink shades, as well as old French roses. Lawrence Johnston eventually retired to France, leaving the gardens to the National Trust.

mother), and so on. Leading off from these are numerous vistas and avenues, framing long and beautiful perspectives.

The main axis of the garden runs from the ancient cedar of Lebanon overlooking the Old Garden (the flower borders in front of the house with a distinctive cottage-garden feel) through the Circle and the famous Red Borders into the Stilt Garden. The Theatre Lawn – the venue for an open-air theatre staged every July – runs parallel on the north side, and it is hedged with immaculate yews.

Critics have sometimes commented on the lack of harmony between the different garden compartments at Hidcote. But all agree that Johnston's planting was so original and innovative that it tends to obscure any real faults the garden might have. Many of Johnston's ideas have been copied and adapted, and so influential has Hidcote been internationally that it is difficult to find a garden of any size in which his ideas have not been used in some form.

HODGES BARN
Shipton Moynes, Tetbury, Gloucestershire

Hodges Barn is a 15th-century structure, built originally as a columbarium, or dovecote. The lofty pale-grey limestone towers and domes were the nesting places for pigeons bred specifically for the table of the local manor. It was 1946 when the present owner's grandmother converted the barn and its site into something more suitable for human habitation. Garden walls were built, terraces made and trees planted; the former dovecote became an engaging family home.

When Charlie and Amanda Hornby took over Hodges Barn 22 years ago they inherited a

RIGHT The water garden is centred on an informal pool, surrounded by moisture-loving plants such as irises, astilbes and *Hosta sieboldiana elegans*, seen here with its soft lilac flowers held aloft on swaying stalks.

mature garden, which they have expanded through much hard work. Now it boasts many garden 'rooms' and walks. Particularly attractive are the vigorous yew specimens, which give a strong introduction to the garden beyond. The eight-acre garden has a relaxed feel, yet everything about it is well defined. The overall

ABOVE In the luscious double rose bed, the Hornbys have planted more than 25 old-fashioned shrub roses, most of which are pale pink or cream in colour. The pale pink modern rose 'Constance Spry' climbs over a wooden pillar while lady's mantle and geraniums provide a vivid contrast at ground level.

impression is of cohesion and a timeless serenity. The Cotswold dry-stone walls that enclose much of the site – built by Italian prisoners of war awaiting repatriation – are smothered in such roses as 'Iceberg', 'Kiftsgate', 'Zéphirine Drouhin', 'Bobbie James', 'Wedding Day' and

ABOVE The tapestry hedge is a powerful architectural feature, providing a backbone to the garden. The hedge is planted with a collection of thuja, holly, beech and yew, a combination that provides interest in both summer and winter.

RIGHT The yew topiary garden opposite the front door of Hodges Barn entices you forward to discover what lies beyond. It is also a particularly effective balance for the house with its twin domes.

'Francis E. Lester'. Charlie Hornby has given full and effective rein to his passion for roses.

The pool and tennis court are well hidden and one comes upon them almost by accident, first passing a tapestry hedge, a combination of thuja, holly, beech and yew. The small water garden, set around an informal pool, is lushly planted with *Thalictrum aquilegifolium* and massed hostas, including a variegated variety that looks very comfortable under the willow.

ABOVE This old metal urn in all its faded glory makes a splendid companion for a free-flowering climbing rose with scarlet double flowers.

RIGHT This view of Hodges Barn shows the perfect symmetry and balance that has been achieved in the planting.

KIFTSGATE COURT
Chipping Campden, Gloucestershire

ABOVE The grand Palladian portico was originally brought from Mickleton Manor in 1887. Its grandeur and scale dominates the terraces and walks of Kiftsgate's gardens. From here, the view across the Vale of Evesham is the Cotswolds at its very best.

RIGHT Against the terrace of the house the terracotta tub overflows with the soft slate-blue mallow, *Malva sylvestris* 'Primley Blue', artemisia and marguerites.

Heather Muir began the garden at Kiftsgate Court in 1918. Lawrence Johnston of Hidcote was her great friend, neighbour and adviser, and there is a lot of Johnston's influence to be seen in the garden. Kiftsgate, however, has a less rigid garden structure than Hidcote, and it is centred on the mellow stone house and its dramatic Cotswold setting.

The grounds at Kiftsgate are an early example of the compartmentalized garden design that is now so popular. The colour-themed 'rooms' are full of surprises, and this is one of the garden's great charms. The overall mood of the garden is very relaxed, and this has been nurtured by three successive generations of Kiftsgate women: Heather Muir's daughter, Diany Binney, and now her granddaughter, Anne Chambers.

Immediately surrounding the house is a series of level walks and terraces. Cauldrons of scarlet verbena and fuchsia blaze on one terrace, while climbing roses such as 'Bleu Magenta' dominate the portico. A few steps down on to the long, curving cross walk, sweeps of pastel pinks, silvers and creams are broken by waves of magenta, deep crimson and carmine within the broad areas of planting.

Beyond the fountain garden, beside the rose walk, is the vast, white-blossomed and fragrant

White roses dominate in the early summer months. Here are *Rosa sericea* 'Heather Muir', named after the owner's grandmother who laid out the original garden at Kiftsgate, and a vast bush of *Rosa soulieana*. The borders are filled with cool, silver-leafed and pastel plants, including santolina and allium.

LEFT The double hedge of the rose garden is a combination of *Rosa gallica* 'Versicolor' and *R. gallica* itself. Dominating the rose garden is the extraordinary specimen of *R. filipes* 'Kiftsgate' – it measures 80 by 90 by 50 feet, and it has eclipsed the copper beech tree on which its climbs.

ABOVE At the end of the famous double hedges of roses is an arch of whitebeam and a modern stone sculpture by Simon Verity, which is, in fact, a seat. This makes a clever structural juxtaposition when seen against the more formal dark green yew hedge behind.

rambler, *Rosa filipes* 'Kiftsgate'. It was planted back in 1938 and still continues to thrive. Further down the hillside there are plantings of citrus, iris and carpenteria to give a Mediterranean feel to that part of the garden. While above, the house and the gigantic pines are silhouetted against a wide, unbroken skyline. Turn around, so that the house is behind you, and you have a breathtaking panorama across the Vale of Evesham.

101

KINGSMEAD
Didmarton, Avon

This house, built in 1720, sits at the edge of an attractive Cotswold village. Its garden has changed considerably from the rose-edged lawn with herbaceous borders it was just 20 years ago. At that time there was also an unruly mass of yew trees, which, with the help of Peter Coats, was transformed into a delightful topiary 'house'. This feature strikes a light-hearted and hospitable note, very much in keeping with the character of the house, and of its owners.

The view across the once unbroken expanse of a huge kitchen garden – formerly a pony paddock – is now interrupted by an octet of clipped conifers and further divided by mown paths. Additionally, a mellow stone wall clothed in climbing roses helps create more of an informal setting.

In another part of the garden is a neatly proportioned 18th-century gazebo with conical roof and colour-washed plaster. The view from the gazebo used to be of a quiet road and occasional horse-drawn carriage. Now, however, a constant stream of traffic has removed the peace and serenity this retreat once offered.

A strong sense of purpose and structure underlies the garden's luxuriant and lavish planting scheme. Featuring prominently among this planting is a wonderful collection of old roses, whose blooms are cut during the summer months to fill the house with colour. But like all good gardens, Kingsmead delights not only the eye, but the nose as well. What could be more perfect as you gaze past the herbaceous border to where horses graze on well-watered pasture?

BELOW Peter Coats and the owners of Kingsmead turned a vast mass of existing yew into an amusing 'house'. The windows and door are framed by wood, with recesses in the yew acting as 'glass'. The effect is one of a particularly witty, living folly. It is also a marvellous example of making the very best out of the raw materials you find when taking on a garden.

LEFT Against the pedimented front of this stuccoed, 18th-century house is an apricot-coloured climbing rose underplanted with large beds of lady's mantle (*Alchemilla mollis*) to provide ground cover.

ABOVE A doorway, complete with a white picket gate, cut into a thick and healthy yew hedge gives access to part of the garden dominated by a witty yew 'house'.

LANGFORD
Lechdale, Oxfordshire

The garden of the Old School House at Langford is the work of royal couturier Sir Hardy Amies. Over the last 20 years, his designer's eye has transformed a disused school playground into an epicurean delight of colour and scent, a desolate patch of weeds into a garden planted with style, grace and panache.

The garden's formal, geometric shapes are especially appealing, and this is particularly noticeable when the grounds are viewed from

BELOW The conical-roofed summerhouse supported by sturdy stone piers is a strong feature in this corner of a lovely stone-walled garden. The box-edged beds brim with peonies, old-fashioned roses and self-seeded foxgloves. The complete look reflects the couturier's sense of line and colour.

ABOVE Sir Hardy Amies created this enchanting village garden from scratch. The ball-topped stone obelisks are a central architectural feature and work well when seen against the profusion of flowers. The combination of old-fashioned roses, dianthus, digitalis, clematis, lavender and rosemary creates a magical effect against the Cotswold stone and the mullioned windows of the house.

above, as Sir Hardy intended. The garden is sheltered from the sometimes troublesome Cotswold winds by walls built of local stone, and these are attractively clothed with old-fashioned roses, double clematis and actinidia. In one corner of the garden stands a dramatic, hexagonal summerhouse, with more old-fashioned roses and heavily scented honeysuckle clambering over its stone supports.

The garden is designed in a very structured, tailored way, with ranks of clipped box providing strong, structural support to beds planted with a wide range of roses, including the deep-crimson 'De Rescht', the striped *Rosa mundi*, the deep puce 'Cardinal de Richelieu' and the cool white 'Madame Hardy'. As a bonus, sweet-scented tobacco plants and herbs such as borage, fennel and sage spill over the disciplined lines with voluptuous abandon in high summer.

In another part of the village Sir Hardy has created a second garden around his tennis court, a garden that is perhaps less conventional and more dynamic in concept. It is here that Sir Hardy struggles with his 'auricula theatre' and foxgloves sow themselves as they wish – all to wonderful effect.

At first sight, the planting at The Old School House seems random and gently cottage-like. However, the combination of pinks, bright and soft, and the contrasting yellow have all been carefully planned for the visual impact both the shape and colour will create.

THE MANOR

Ablington, Bilbury, Gloucestershire

The Manor was built in 1590 for John Coxwell, a wool merchant, and its stone walls still retain the original local yellow ochre limewash stucco. The Manor's charming and original porch exhibits a mixture of both classical and traditional Cotswold motifs.

The present owner, Robert Cooper, has lived at The Manor for 21 years, but when he moved in there was virtually no garden. The only feature of any merit was a clump of old yew trees, which had been half-heartedly clipped into a rather formless shape.

Over the years, Robert Cooper has imposed structure and form on the garden. He denies that there ever was a 'master plan', and insists that the garden simply 'evolved', with the help of his gardener Lesley Blackwell. Today, both the house and garden work in harmony with the ravishing setting. In May, the south face of the house is covered in mauve wisteria and the terrace, which is flanked by weeping pear trees, looks across a lawn reclaimed from moss to the River Coln. You cross the river using a handsome bridge, walking under a new wisteria-clad

BELOW The bird is a classic Roman topiary shape. The other was inspired by Henry Moore's sculptures. In the foreground you can see massed cream-coloured delphiniums, which look divine against the lush green yew. The gabled, stuccoed house provides yet another contrast.

ABOVE Robert Cooper built this simple wooden bridge across the River Coln, and it is thoughtfully designed to seem a part of the tranquil, undisturbed setting. The stone summerhouse, which takes full advantage of this picturesque spot, has a moss-covered stone roof that gives it a timeless appearance.

LEFT The enchanting, stone-built summerhouse with its Gothic-style windows sits beside the River Coln. The twisted trunks of the standard bay trees add a touch of whimsy to this delightful scene.

109

pergola, to the Elizabethan-inspired hip-roofed gazebo, which looks back up to the house.

About nine years ago, Robert Cooper built a walled garden by the house and Rosemary Verey planted up two of its large borders. The garden now has a peaceful 'Englishness' about it, and the combination of old-fashioned roses, clematis and peonies is most pleasing. The whole effect of this gentle garden is one of balance and serenity.

ABOVE This stone gazebo was built by The Manor's owner two years ago. It is inspired by Elizabethan architecture and looks back across the River Coln to the stone terrace and path, flanked by the strong shapes of golden yew, which were planted at the turn of the century. The perspective here has a balanced, architectural look to it.

RIGHT When the present owner, Robert Cooper, moved to The Manor, there were no paths, walks, or garden structure of any kind, except for this mass of yew. Over the last 21 years, he has shaped the yew so that it now looks Jacobean in concept. The pale stone gazebo, although only two years old, looks as if it has always stood on this spot.

MANOR FARM
Minster Lovell, Oxfordshire

When Lady Parker first saw Manor Farm 20 years ago, she was enchanted by its potential. At that time, however, both the house and garden were completely derelict. The house was an 11th-century monastic building, parts of which remain in the structure that was rebuilt in the 15th century as the farmhouse for the local manor, which now stands in ruins nearby on the banks of the Windrush River.

The farmhouse's orchard adjoins the fine cruciform parish church, and a beautiful 15th-century circular dovecote overlooks both the

RIGHT St Kenelm's church is a 15th-century cruciform building that is still used today. The rambling rose *Rosa filipes* 'Kiftsgate' hangs from a wall, in the crevices of which grow thyme, rock roses and poppies.

LEFT On one of the many original old stone walls, the rigid, upright climbing rose 'Paul's Lemon Pillar' provides a soft background to the dramatic purple-crimson shrub rose 'Gypsy Boy', with the added bonus of its double, lemon-white scented flowers. Lady Parker has used roses as a unifying theme throughout the garden.

RIGHT Wonderful, bold pink 'Président de Sèze' roses flank the drive to Manor Farm. When creating the garden, Lady Parker integrated the farm buildings that surround the house into the garden itself. Rather than making a series of garden 'rooms', she decided to create a unified garden, and even moved walls to ensure that there would be uninterrupted views.

upper and lower pools. Although very recent additions, the pools look as though they have always been there. Lady Parker admits to making some terrible mistakes, but she was right to use the site's existing features, such as the old stone walls and the farm buildings, as the basis for the structure of the garden. The old tractor sheds were stripped of their unattractive tin roofs, leaving just the skeletal beams and pillars on view to form an arcade in an area that has become known as Arcadia. At first, the hard-packed soil around Arcadia was distinctly unfriendly to plants, but after a lot of hard work the pillars you see there today are swathed in climbing roses and honeysuckle.

Lady Parker confesses that many of her design innovations were motivated by impatience rather than planning, but she has kept the garden informal in the belief that anything too grand would be somehow inappropriate for a farmhouse. Although the planting is simple, it is not symmetrical, and everywhere you look there is a sense of balance, with enough surprises to delight the eye.

THE OLD CHAPEL
Chalford, Stroud, Gloucestershire

Eight years ago, John and Fiona Owen moved into their Wesleyan chapel, built in 1857 from the locally available Cotswold stone. At that time, there was no garden or vehicular access of any description, and Fiona Owen remembers it as 'a 30-feet-high cliff with a bonfire site in the middle of it'.

Within six years, however, the 'cliff' had four terraces linked by stone steps made by John Owen, and Fiona estimates that they had brought in seven tons of gravel and top soil, all without the aid of vehicles.

Both John and Fiona Owen are artists and they divided their time between the garden and their work. They started at the main level, upon which the house sits, and expanded the garden until their vertical acre had been transformed into a haven of colour and billowing borders. John has built all the 'architectural things' in the garden himself.

They both like and admire the principles underlying the 19th-century Arts and Crafts Movement, and the 10-feet-high stone tower –

John's Folly – on the highest terrace overlooking the valley below is the culmination of all his projects in stone.

The entire garden has been designed as an allegory for the journey through life. The borders have been planted to give a tapestry-like effect, which Fiona Owen says is 'not fashionable and not grand, but they create a mood'. The different colours and shades symbolize the different ages of Man. The Owens have made a garden for the pure pleasure it gives them and, in so doing, have tamed an extraordinarily difficult site and turned it into something unique and remarkable.

BELOW The owners call this secluded peaceful area 'the retreat'. The summerhouse was inspired by a mixture of Eastern culture and the Arts and Crafts Movement. The Gothic-style bench was copied from one of Fiona Owen's paintings. The temple bell was originally from Tibet, the urn from Thailand and the pots are planted with maples. Clumps of gardener's garters, primulas and iris thrive around the pond.

LEFT The Contemplation Garden at the Old Chapel is planted on the topmost terrace. John Owen brought every stone up to this level by hand to build his folly. The iron obelisks frame a bench in the middle of the garden and the borders overflow with allium, iris and massed sweet rocket.

ABOVE This bird house in the Victorian High-Gothic style was made by a local craftsman from one of Fiona Owen's sketches. It sits on the third level of the Old Chapel garden, surrounded by an orchard and old-fashioned shrub roses, such as the double *Rosa californica* and *R.* 'Blanch Double de Coubert'.

115

PAINSWICK ROCOCO GARDEN

Painswick, Gloucestershire

Painswick is situated on a high spur between two valleys. Cut off from the surrounding countryside is the Painswick Rococo Garden — a secret, hidden place and an intimate retreat of great charm.

The story of the Painswick restoration is as fascinating as the garden itself. The work started in 1984 and continues today. The initial reference was Thomas Robbins' detailed paintings of 1748 of the house and garden for Benjamin Hyett, who inherited the house in 1738 and established the gardens. It is Hyett's descendant, Lord Dickinson, who inherited the estate in 1958 and initiated the restoration.

When the restoration work commenced the garden was covered in brambles, saplings and fallen trees. Initial investigation revealed, however, that the layout and many of the garden buildings, seen in Robbins' paintings, had survived the centuries of neglect.

ABOVE A view of the Exedra Garden, named after the new exedra (an outside seating place) that was copied from a detail in one of the paintings by Robbins. Its Gothic screen is sited near the excavated top pond and is made of painted wood and plaster around a steel frame. New plantings of hornbeam will eventually grow to form a hedge on either side.

RIGHT The Snowdrop Grove in the woods to the west of the garden was once a jungle. Now it is home to the most beautiful carpet of snowdrops in late winter. Here nature holds sway and Pope would have thought it a wonderful example of 'the amiable Simplicity of unadorned Nature'.

A door of the Gothic-styled Red House, so called because it was originally painted that colour, commands a fine view of the main part of the garden – west to the fish pond and the woods beyond. The folly lies to the north of the main garden area and has two façades angled to face different vistas.

One of the guiding principles underlying the restoration has been to site all features precisely as they originally were, since they are so closely interrelated. All rely heavily on a path, for example, or a garden building or a vista to make any particular part work in harmony with the whole. This is perhaps what is most exciting about the garden. Another important consideration is that this is an extremely fine example of a transitional garden, somewhere between a strictly formal approach and the full-blown naturalism of Capability Brown.

The replanting is now well under way and much of the building and path restoration is complete. The distinctive character of Painswick – its small-scale intimacy – has been reinstated.

THE PRIORY
Charlbury, Oxfordshire

The Priory is a village house set in seven acres of Cotswold countryside. Originally, in the 12th century, the Priory was the monastic court for the abbots of Eynsham, but the building now sports relatively recent, 17th-century, additions. By the mid-19th century, the Shilsons, local wool merchants, had bought the house and in the 1930s the family commissioned the formal gardens and topiary that can be seen today.

In 1987, the present owners – a group of London doctors who work with the homeless at Wytham Hall, Maida Vale – bought the Priory. They do not employ a professional gardener; instead each works in the garden and any decisions concerning overall planning and design are made by consensus. As a result of their work, the neglected beds are now a thing of the past, and while the formal gardens still survive, these have been incorporated into more Italianate arrangements.

There is a real focus to the garden at the Priory. It is designed to be a contemplative space and an inscription found inside a small stone temple reads 'Eternity is in love with the productions of time', which is a line from William Blake's *The Marriage of Heaven and Hell*. The Temple Garden is a perfect setting, with specimen trees and double rows of standard junipers, shaped into globes.

The doctors see the garden is an extension of the way they look at life. The pale foliage, the gentle colours and the overriding green-on-green architecture brings order, clarity and beauty to this garden.

The stone paths and yew hedges are part of the new work in this part of the garden, undertaken within the last five years. Eventually, these will create more garden 'rooms'. The middle distance is dominated by clipped, domed tunnels of yew, which were planted in the 1930s.

Sunlight falls warmly on the Chilstone Temple, which is the focus of the Temple Garden. The double rows of standard clipped junipers echo the Temple's shape. This garden room is also planted with rare specimen plants and trees, including Japanese black bamboo, several Japanese maples and a weeping cedar.

The columnar yews in the Italian Garden were planted when the formal gardens were first laid out in the 1930s. The original stone piers and yew tunnel beyond lend their structure to this part of the garden. The focus of the garden is the variation of green-on-green, while the canal balances the perpendicular yews.

RODMARTON MANOR
Cirencester, Gloucestershire

The Barnsley-designed Rodmarton Manor is an Arts and Crafts vision realized in the Cotswolds. Every piece of stone and wood was fashioned by local craftsman using raw materials from the estate. The grey stone house rises tall behind the closely clipped topiary.

The Terrace at Rodmarton has a rigidly trimmed yew hedge, which provides both structure and protection from the wind. The blue agapanthus is a strong contrast against the dark green yews, as is the Victorian scissor-backed garden seat. The box topiary garden is situated beyond the hedge to the left.

Between 1909 and 1926 the architect Ernest Barnsley and his client Claud Biddulph built and furnished Rodmarton Manor, using material from the estate. The house and gardens sit high on the Cotswold hills, enjoying distant views of the Marlborough Downs and its construction was the finest achievement of the Cotswold Tradition, whose origins lay in William Morris's Arts and Crafts Movement.

It was Barnsley who is responsible for the design of the garden, and he used as his guiding principle the idea that both the house and garden should be linked in style and should resonate with the wider landscape. Thus, at Rodmarton, the order and symmetry nearest the house gradually give way to informality, and finally to uncontrived nature in the Wild Garden. Barnsley designed the garden as a series

of 'rooms', with hedges and Cotswold dry-stone walls forming the boundaries of each separate area of garden.

Inevitably, the garden has been compared with Hidcote and Sissinghurst, but it has more of an international character and some of its features are uniquely Rodmarton. Most impressive are the oversized topiary chairs of yew, with yew backs and arms and stone seats. These are to be found amidst the herbaceous borders. Their structure and visual focus on a small, stone-edged pool is both witty and imaginative.

When Mary and Anthony Biddulph inherited the house in 1955, it was Mary who set about bringing the garden back from the state of neglect it had fallen into during the war. Now the next generation has embarked on a scheme of restoration and replanting.

ROUSHAM HOUSE
Steeple Aston, Oxfordshire

Rousham House has one of the most famous 18th-century gardens in Europe. It is remarkable in that it has not been substantially altered since it was created by William Kent in the 1730s. This is due to the fact that the house and its gardens have remained in the Cottrell-Dormer family for the last 265 years.

In Kent's work at Rousham one sees simplicity of design as an end in itself. His judicious use of the finest classical sculpture and his understanding of classical architecture in the buildings he designed for Rousham make a strong statement. The different greens against the cool stone structures give form and line. This is no flower-dominated garden with burgeoning borders.

Kent used curves in the garden as a reflection of the favoured serpentine line of the fashionable Rococo style of the 1730s. His garden circuit is precise and as you retrace his steps, you can appreciate the contrasts and distinct areas that merge one into the other. He understood how pleasing it is to come from light into shade, from dense planting to open spaces, to hear water playing over stone. Water is used in all its forms at Rousham – even the River Cherwell becomes the focal point for several Kent buildings within this 25-acre garden.

Rousham is simply a delight. Kent has juxtaposed plants with statues and buildings in a successful attempt to crystallize the 18th-century notion of harmony between Man and Nature.

Rousham was originally built in 1635 and then remodelled in 1738 by William Kent. The building is now seen as the definitive Kent work, since no detail of the house, garden, garden buildings or statuary was ignored. Here, the stone urn in the foreground frames the Kent-remodelled house while long-horned cattle graze in the winter landscape.

LEFT The Pigeon House Garden takes its name from the early 17th-century circular dovecote within the 17th-century walled garden. The box-edged parterres create a pattern which is effective year-round.

ABOVE In this summer view of the Pigeon House Garden, the geometric, box-edged parterres edged with gravel paths are planted with red valerian and pastel pink roses.

ABOVE From the Praeneste (a stone arcade of seven pedimented arches inside which are alcoves for statues and seats designed by Kent) the view is across the River Cherwell in the valley below to the 'eye-catcher' – a false ruin on the horizon.

RIGHT On the edge of the slope is this dramatic stone sculpture of a horse being attacked by a lion by Scheemakers. Behind it is a trellised arbour, one of a pair designed by William Kent for Rousham.

ABOVE The placement of every statue is an important part of the detail of Kent's vision for Rousham. Here Pan, the god of nature, is sited at the bottom of the Cascade of Venus. It is a tranquil area in which to pause and reflect, especially when the evergreens of Rousham take on their winter mantle of white.

RIGHT A view through the imaginative 18th-century wrought-iron gate looking into the walled garden. If only modern wrought-iron makers would use this as a model, I would perhaps become a convert to this material.

SEZINCOTE
Moreton-in-Marsh, Gloucestershire

Sezincote was completed in 1815. Its architecture was inspired by the owners' years oversees with the East India Company. The house is built of local Cotswold stone and has a commanding position with breathtaking views across the Evenlode Valley to the hills. It is, however, no ordinary Cotswold mansion. With its onion-shaped domes, peacock-tail arched windows and small minarets, it is rather a nabob's house.

Samuel Pepys Cockerell, the brother of the owner, was the architect of this startling Cotswold structure, which is said to have inspired the later Brighton Pavilion after the Prince Regent saw it in 1806. The artist Thomas Daniell, who had spent eight years in India, advised on both the house and the garden and designed the exotic bridge, originally topped with cast-iron Brahmin bulls, and the temple to Surya, the Hindu sun god, which stands above the Thornery north of the house. The garden architect Humphrey Repton, the successor to Capability Brown, was consulted on the general layout of the gardens, the shape of the serpentine lake and the planting of the woodland. Later, in the 1960s, Graham Stuart Thomas and Lady Kleinwort devised much of the planting.

With the overwhelming Eastern influence of the house so much in evidence, Sezincote's garden is a curious, most successful, combination of idyllic 18th-century parkland and the exotic. The original framework of the garden boasts trees that were planted before 1818 and are still growing today, including four huge cedars of Lebanon to be found near the rock pool, and a weeping hornbeam thought to be the largest of its kind in England.

Water has always played an important part in the area to the north of the house. Here, the water gardens are known as the Thornery. The temple to Surya overlooks the first of a string of pools that lie one below another, linked by streams and cascades.

RIGHT The curving orangery is a strong background to the Paradise Garden, planted as a traditional Mogul garden in 1965. The fastigiate yews and canals divide the south lawn into four equal parts, representing the four rivers of life, and the central pond is symbolic of the meeting of humanity and God.

OVERLEAF The Brahmin bulls positioned by the temple to Surya and on the bridge were originally made of Coade 'stone'. However, when the stone started to disintegrate, faithful replicas in cast iron were made to replace them.

Around the Snake Pool with the Daniell bridge above, a realistic metal snake slithers up a trunk of dead yew and the planting around the edges echoes the dappled surroundings. There is a great clump of Chinese bamboo here as well as plentiful hydrangeas, and bright rock roses, primulas, irises, lilies, hostas, astilbes and tree peonies border the pools that form as the stream meanders eastwards.

In 1965 Graham Thomas and Lady Kleinwort collaborated in the creation of the imposing Paradise Garden, which now lies below the sweeping curve of the delicate Indian orangery beside the house. It is modelled on traditional Mogul Paradise Gardens. Its planting is symbolic and the lawn is crossed by canals that meet at a central pond. From here, variegated ivy, bergenia and the large-leafed *Vitis coignetiae* decorate the flights of steps that lead up to the original grotto and tennis pavilion.

A splendid arc of trees shelters this part of the garden, with copper beeches underplanted with dogwoods gleaming within the mystical setting of Sezincote, a remarkable mixture of East and West, which Sir John Betjeman hailed as 'Exotic Sezincote! Stately and strange'.

SHEEPBRIDGE BARN
Eastleach, Gloucestershire

Approximately fifteen hundred years ago, Sheepbridge Barn was the site of a Roman staging post. This explains why the house, a converted 17th-century Cotswold stone barn, boasts a colonnade of Roman pillars. This colonnade forms a most romantic feature for the house and garden and, with the warm stone of the house itself, is the best possible backdrop for this essentially green-on-green garden.

When Sir Guy and Lady Holland moved here 20 years ago, they first had to excavate deep trenches in the garden and then fill them with imported local soil. This was to allow the plants to put their roots down over a two-feet layer of stone that was once a Roman cattleyard.

Ringed by many wonderful old beeches, which act as a shelter belt for this rather exposed site, the garden is now an example of enormous

ABOVE LEFT Planted close to the converted 17th-century Cotswold barn is a series of clipped topiary designs. The glossy dark green foliage of the box (*Buxus sempervirens*) is shaped in September or October to maintain the disciplined effect.

discipline, although Sir Guy maintains it is not labour intensive. Beautifully clipped combinations of box make strong statements when seen against the converted barn, and the perpendicular Portuguese laurel buttressing the walls is a treat. Although the box has been clipped to different heights and shapes, the severity of their forms, and their relationship to each other, produce a strikingly harmonious effect.

Where there are borders in the garden, these have been densely planted with low-growing, vigorous plants, such as lady's mantle (*Alchemilla mollis*) and hostas, and all colours – apart from greens and whites – have been banished from the garden.

ABOVE Vegetative buttresses of Portuguese laurel appear to support the end stone wall of the 17th-century converted barn. The owner, Sir Guy Holland, clips and shapes all the plants himself within his one-acre garden.

STANCOMBE PARK
Stinchcombe, Gloucestershire

Stancombe Park lies at the head of a Cotswold valley, below Stinchcombe Hill. It is an imposing Regency house with some later Victorian influences. The garden here is in two distinct parts. The first, nearest the house, has been created from parkland. Moving up a yew-lined flight of stone steps, you come upon four box-edged borders dramatically framed by yew hedges. An inlaid scroll pattern of low box hedging creates circular and curved beds within the rectangles. Each bed is planted in a particular colour: one blue, one red and two in shades of yellow.

Close to these colour-themed beds, in the middle of the upper lawn, can be found another classical feature – a circular planting of maples (*Acer pseudoplatanus* 'Worleei') surrounding an enormous marble urn hedged with box and privet. Through an opening in the maples, a

ABOVE This large marble urn is surrounded by a circle of shaped box and privet, within the circular planting of maples, making a coherent design statement.

RIGHT This classical pavilion overlooks the crystal-clear lake fed by a natural spring. The path leading down to the water is edged with shaped box hedges.

ABOVE The 19th-century wrought-iron gates and low stone walls, topped with charming stone vases, divide the house and the more formal gardens from the parkland beyond. Low-growing lady's mantle spreads itself leisurely around the base of the attractive walls and gates.

LEFT These mismatched propagating houses are said to have been the rendezvous for the Reverend Edwards and his lover in the early 19th century. There are banks of maples and buddleias while the pathway is flanked by box. The icehouse roof here incorporates the jawbone of a whale that had become stranded and died in the nearby Severn.

pleached lime walk leads to another of the garden's set-pieces. Within a white, Chinese Chippendale-style fence is a white bench of similar style. This bench is flanked by four cherubs and all is surrounded with *Osmanthus delavayi* and masses of old-fashioned shrub and rambling roses.

Dense plantings of shrubs define the narrow, steep stone path that leads down to the extraordinary Folly Garden, the second part of the garden at Stancombe. On the way are two lakes and a font partly obscured by a rambling hydrangea and featuring a mosaic of Roman origin – from a largely unexcavated Roman villa in a nearby wood.

Within the Folly Garden the path forks right, leading into a jungle-like area of plants, such as the extravagant *Gunnera manicata*, standing at shoulder height. The path narrows here and the whole experience of Stancombe suddenly becomes High Gothic. A dimly lit tunnel guarded by a huge stone dog is the only way forward. The tunnel zigs and zags through tight, dark passages until, at the very end, there is a chink of light from a medieval-style slit window. On

An informal scene at Stancombe, looking towards a farm cottage, with the striking, columnar shapes of Irish yews dividing the space. The white foxgloves and the pastel shades of campanulas and alliums combine to produce a restful atmosphere.

peering through, you are rewarded by a sight of pure magic – a calm, placid lake and a beautifully sited Doric temple.

The Folly Garden was established sometime at the beginning of the 19th century. Tradition has it that the then owner, the Reverend David Edwards, had a wealthy and very oversized wife. In order that she never discover his liaison with an attractive local girl, the narrow tunnels were made as the only means of entering the Folly Garden, which was their secret meeting place. Whether or not this is the true explanation for this wondrous garden does not really matter.

The Folly Garden has simply become a part of the eccentricity that is Stancombe.

Another example of Stancombe's eccentricity can be seen near the lake – a magnificent pair of mismatched, early 19th-century domed propagating houses – one of which with a whale's jawbone for an entrance.

Stancombe has been maintained and developed by Gerda and the late Basil Barlow since they moved to the house in 1964. Peter Coats, a family friend, helped devise the planting, but it is now Gerda's vision alone that sustains this remarkable garden.

In the Pattern Border are box-edged beds clipped to form a Baroque-inspired design. The garden is punctuated by dramatic wings of yew, which, although only six years old, give the garden a very definite structure. In between the box-edging, each bed is planted with flowers.

141

STOWELL PARK
Northleach, Gloucestershire

Stowell Park commands a spectacular view across the beautiful Cotswolds Coln Valley. The house was built in the 17th century, but it was Sir John Belcher's 19th-century additions for Lord Eldon that laid down the 'bones' of the present garden. The stone balustrading of the terraces and the walled garden with its original and beautifully restored peach houses remain major features today.

The Vestey family has owned Stowell Park since the 1920s. However, the formal borders and immaculate kitchen gardens were very much in the old gardening tradition. When Lady Vestey moved to Stowell Park more than a decade ago, she dreamed of creating a softer, English country garden, one that enhanced the magnificent setting. She was fortunate to discovering a tremendous plantsman in her head gardener, Neil Hewertson, and together they have used the existing architectural features of the garden as the basic framework for a wide-ranging and imaginative planting scheme,

BELOW A pleached lime avenue planted in 1983 leads from the pair of stone gate-houses built in 1880 to the imposing house, which seems to glow in the afternoon sun. In the beds immediately in front of the house, Lady Vestey has indulged her passion for roses, among them are 'Jacques Cartier' and 'Ispahan'.

ABOVE The house and gardens at Stowell Park command an unparalleled view across the Coln Valley to the Chedworth Woods and beyond. It is because of the vast scale of the setting that Lady Vestey has rightly used a bold, simple planting scheme. The evergreen box in the urns has replaced fussy annuals and the roses in the foreground provide an informal counterpoint.

changing the character of the gardens while strengthening the relationship of the house and garden to the wider landscape.

The pale grey stone of the house and balustrading are softened by climbers and roses. The over-fussy planting has gone, and now yew buttresses are shaped against a long, high stone wall to provide year-round form and interest. A rose pergola divides the walled garden, thus making the peach house a focal point. Here, too, is a ravishing border, cleverly marked out with shaped yew. Lady Vestey's understanding of the importance of scale and the bold, simple planting dictate the essence of the garden.

SUDELEY CASTLE
Winchcombe, Gloucestershire

The history of Sudeley Castle is long and fascinating. From the 15th century it maintained royal connections and in 1547 its then owner, Sir Thomas Seymour, brought his new wife Queen Katherine Parr, widow of Henry VIII, to Sudeley. With her was her protégé, the tragic Lady Jane Grey, who was to become Queen for nine days in 1553. Queen Katherine Parr died in childbirth in 1548 and is buried in St Mary's Chapel.

The castle and chapel were badly damaged in the Civil War and then neglected for two centuries, until the Dent brothers undertook an ambitious restoration programme in the 19th century. The new gardens were laid out around the old ruins and the centrepiece is undoubtedly the Queen's Garden. Planted in the 1850s on the site of the original Tudor parterre, it is lush and extravagant. Today there are 800 roses underplanted with aromatic herbs and in summer the scents and colours literally assault the senses.

The peaceful Tithe Barn Garden is almost overwhelmed by wisteria in May, a sight enhanced when seen reflected in the nearby carp pond. The Chapel Border Garden is another attractive feature of Sudeley Castle. Its yellow, white and purple planting is soft and informal and the huge white heads of hydrangea around the door of St Mary's Chapel are ravishing.

The present owner, Lady Ashcombe, believes that the gardens are a vital part of the future of Sudeley Castle. She says of her work: 'I see the planting as an embellishment to the history of the house.'

The Queen's Garden is divided into quarters, each emphasized by medieval herbs grown in edged segments of a circle. In summer the geometry of the circles is lost as a profusion of roses tumbles over the edges.

The emphasis here is on historical plants, but perpetual-flowering roses, such as 'William Shakespeare', bloom long after the 19th-century roses, such as 'Madame Isaac Péreire' and 'Comte de Chambord', have ended.

LEFT Sir Thomas Seymour refurbished the Castle when he married Queen Katherine Parr. This is the private garden Lady Ashcombe has planted within the internal courtyard of the two wings built from the original gatehouse, which now forms the house.

LEFT St Mary's Chapel, built in the 15th century, was looted and destroyed during the Civil War. It was restored by Sir Giles Gilbert Scott, who also designed Queen Katherine Parr's tomb within the chapel. The tall yew hedges give the surrounding gardens an enclosed, intimate harmony, and the old-fashioned climbing roses look charming against the ancient stones of the building.

ABOVE The ruins of the tithe barn, which was built by the first Baron Sudeley in the mid-15th century and destroyed by Cromwell. It is now a peaceful garden incorporating a carp pond, and in May the old stone ruins are covered in wisteria.

WESTWELL MANOR

Burford, Gloucestershire

Westwell is a delightful Cotswold hamlet in the Windrush valley, and the village itself is named after the well to be found in the grounds of Westwell Manor. The house, in essence, is 16th century, with an additional wing constructed in 1718. Thereafter, the Manor's different owners over the years have added to or subtracted from it.

The structure of the present-day seven-acre garden was laid out at the beginning of this century by Sir Sothern and Lady Holland, both of whom were notable amateur gardeners, and Westwell remained in the Holland family until 1975. So, when the present owners, Anthea and Thomas Gibson, moved to Westwell in 1979, they took over an established garden with gates, fine 18th-century walls, established structuring hedges, low walls, paving and topiary – all a wonderful legacy from the Holland family's time at Westwell.

It is Anthea Gibson who is the garden-maker of the family, and it is she who has taken the good bones of the garden and enhanced and enlarged them. Her approach to the garden has been essentially disciplined and strong, and she has executed her vision with a sure hand and an informed eye.

One of the first things Anthea Gibson set about correcting was the scale of the grass walk between two existing, enormously wide herbaceous borders. She widened this walk, thus reducing the width of the borders, and laid down mowing stones to make maintenance easier. Now the borders are properly centred on the house in one direction and, in another, an existing gate has been moved to enhance a wall opening in order to create an equally strong architectural focal point. In this way, she has achieved a pleasing balance with the minimum of effort and expense.

The original topiary garden was established close to the house and planted with specimens brought from Holland by Sir Sothern back in 1920. The abstract yew and box, the shaped peacocks, finials and spirals all combine to underline the house's Elizabethan origins. Both

LEFT This old wisteria covers a stone-pillared pergola and it was probably planted by Sir Sothern Holland. The long fragrant racemes of mauve flowers are at their best in May and June. This pergola is adjacent to the Lily Pond Garden and close to the Water Garden, making it a favoured spot in summer.

ABOVE The double herbaceous borders which line the path leading up to the house are planted in the tradition of true herbaceous borders. They are planted intelligently and give interest for nine months of the year

the house and the garden share an architectural framework that stresses their unity. Thus, Westwell's garden uses the conceits of an earlier age, when living evergreen sculpture provided wit in the garden.

The recently planted circular Full Moon Garden 'room', as its name implies, is designed to be enjoyed by moonlight, and so it utilizes predominantly grey and silver foliage. Formal clipped standards are to be found in many of the garden rooms and everywhere the attention to detail is apparent, such as in the black-painted swimming pool.

The marvellous ornamental vegetable garden – planted eight years ago – is functional as well as decorative, and the produce from this area of Westwell are enjoyed by the family all year round. Yet even here, there is a strong underlying design structure. Box-edged beds surround four standard evergreen Portuguese laurels, and

The Topiary Garden was planted in 1920 by Sir Sothern Holland using specimens he imported from Holland. This part of the house was originally the stables and the stone arch was the entrance to the stableyard. The present owner has planted a small box topiary in front of the other wing of the house in the Sundial Garden.

connecting paths are attractively brick-paved. A wooden arbour has also been built to act as a focal point for the garden. On this, roses climb in summer, and there are also herbs, lavender and trial beds. This is definitely a working kitchen garden, but one that is orderly, immensely practical, and full of style.

These topiary shapes and strong yew edges are part of the early 20th-century input from Sir Sothern Holland. The abstract shapes are not always symmetrical, but the effect is of Jacobean garden topiary. At the foot of the abstract masonry, Anthea Gibson has introduced the stronger-coloured yellow plants she intrinsically likes but can use only sparingly in the rest of the garden.

153

WOOTTON PLACE
Oxfordshire

When the current owners first saw Wootton Place six years ago, they fell in love at once with the old walled garden with its typical Cotswold outbuildings, including stone stables and attached dovecote, complete with doves. There is also a granary sited at the rear of the Georgian house.

Four acres of mature garden and a further ten acres of parkland surround the house. Capability Brown is believed to have laid out the parkland, which still boasts some splendid old cedars, copper beeches, and a mulberry and walnut tree from the 18th century. The garden's strongest features, however, are its borders and the walled garden, which are thought to date from the late 19th and early 20th centuries.

Within the mile of dry-stone walling that surrounds the house and parkland, the garden is complete within itself, not relying on views, individual garden 'rooms' or spectacular settings for its impact. Instead, it flows gently from the house over one level to the distant parkland.

Bordering tranquil stretches of grass are long, broad herbaceous borders, intensely planted with poppies, geraniums, potentillas, peonies and roses. Their cottage-garden colours of pink, white and blue work together beautifully in this deceptively simple layout. The walled garden is reminiscent of some secret garden: old roses grow thickly over wooden tripods and ancient apple trees stand without formality, while plum and pear trees are fanned along the walls.

Although the scale of the garden at Wootton Place is grand, it is unpretentious and, above all, charming and romantic.

There is a timeless quality to the garden at Wootton Place. Here, in the orchard that borders the more formal gardens, drifts of scilla mingle with daffodils in early spring under an apple tree. Beyond this peaceful corner, there are ten acres of parkland thought to have been laid out in the 18th century by Capability Brown.

LIST OF GARDENS

GARDENS NOT OPEN TO THE PUBLIC

Mr David and Lady Pamela Hicks
The Grove
Brightwell Baldwin
Oxon

Dikler Farming Co.
Abbotswood
Stow-in-Wold
Gloucestershire

The Duke of Beaufort
Badminton
Avon

The Earl and Countess Cairns
Bolehyde Manor
Wiltshire

Mr and Mrs R. Paice
Bourton House
Bourton-on-the-Hill
Gloucestershire

Mr and Mrs D. Hodges
Brook Cottage
Alkerton
Oxfordshire

The Lord Saye and Sele
Broughton Castle
Oxfordshire

The Hon. Peter Ward
Cornwell Manor
Oxfordshire

Daylesford House
Daylesford
Gloucestershire

Mr James Lees-Milne
Essex House
Great Badminton
Chipping Sodbury
Avon

Jane, Countess of Westmorland
Kingsmead
Didmarton
Avon

Mr Robert Cooper
The Manor
Ablington
Bilbury
Oxfordshire

Fiona and John Owen
The Old Chapel
Chalford
Stroud
Gloucestershire

Dr el Kabir
The Priory
Charlbury
Oxfordshire

Sir Guy and Lady Holland
Sheepbridge Barn
Eastleach
Cirencester
Gloucestershire

The Lord and Lady Vestey
Stowell Park
Northleach
Gloucestershire

Mr and Mrs H. Dyer
Wootton Place
nr Woodstock
Oxfordshire

GARDENS OPEN TO THE PUBLIC
(Details available on application)

Mr Guy and the Hon. Mrs Acloque
Alderley Grange
Wotton-under-Edge
Gloucestershire
GL12 7QT
Tel: (01453) 842 161

Rosemary Verey
Barnsley House
Cirencester
Gloucestershire
GL7 5EE
Tel: (01285) 740 281

The Duke of Marlborough
Blenheim Palace
Woodstock
Oxford
OX20 1PX
Tel: (01993) 811 091

The National Trust
Buscot Park
Farringdon
Oxfordshire
SN7 8BU
Tel: (01367) 242 094

Denny Wickham & Peter Fox
Clock House
Coleshill
Swindon
Wiltshire
Tel: (01793) 762 476

The Ditchley Foundation
Ditchley Park
Enstone
Chipping Norton
Oxfordshire
OX7 4ER
Tel: (01608) 677 346
Visits by prior arrangement with
the Bursar – Monday, Tuesday
and Thursday afternoons only

Mr and Mrs Andrew Lawson
Gothic House
Charlbury
Oxfordshire
Tel: (01608) 810 654

The National Trust
Hidcote Manor Garden
Gloucestershire
GL55 6LR
Tel: (01386) 438 333

Mr and Mrs Charles Hornby
Hodges Barn
Shipton Moyne
Gloucestershire

Mr and Mrs J. G. Chambers
Kiftsgate Court
Chipping Campden
Gloucestershire
GL55 6LW
Tel: (01386) 438 777

Sir Hardy Amies
The Old School
Langford
Nr. Lechlade
Gloucestershire
GL7 3LF
Tel: 01367860-283

Sir Peter and Lady Parker
The Manor Farm
Minster Lovell
Oxfordshire

Mr and Mrs Simon Biddulph
Rodmarton Manor
Cirencester
Gloucestershire
GL7 6PF
Tel: (01285) 841 253/278

Painswick Rococo Garden Trust
Painswick Rococo Gardens
Gloucestershire
Tel: (01452) 813 204

Mrs Basil Barlow
Stancombe Park
Dursley
Gloucestershire
GL11 6AU
Tel: (01453) 542 815

The Lady Ashcombe
Sudeley Castle
Winchcombe
Gloucestershire
GL54 5JD
Tel: (01242) 602 308

Mr and Mrs Cottrell-Dormer
Rousham House
Steeple Aston
Oxon
OX5 3QX
Tel: (01869) 471 10

Mr and Mrs David Peake
Sezincote
Moreton-in-Marsh
Gloucestershire
GL56 9AW

Mr and Mrs Thomas Gibson
Westwell Manor
Near Burford
Oxfordshire
OX18 4JT
Fax: (01993) 824090

INDEX